THESE THINGS YOU OUGHT TO KNOW

THESE THINGS YOU OUGHT TO KNOW

MIKE EASTER

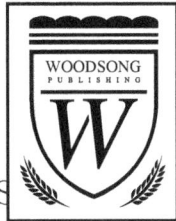

These Things You Ought To Know
Mike Easter

Cover design: Vision Graphics, Seymour, IN

Edited by Patricia Bollmann

Printed in the United States of America

ISBN: 978-1-7349323-3-1

Table of Contents

Preface

Some things are vital to know. For instance, here are a few examples drawn from a list of fifty important things people ought to know. The list was compiled by Brian Lee, chief of product management at Lifehack:

- Don't stop learning: If you start coasting through life, you're gonna lose. Always stretch your intellect.
- Forgive as much as possible. Grudges achieve little.
- Do something that's not for money.
- Time passes by a lot faster than you'd think. This effect accelerates with age.
- Some things can't be learned; they can only be experienced.
- Wealth is relatively unimportant.
- Don't lie to yourself.
- Wealth is measured by your happiness and not by your financial statement.
- Learn to handle criticism.
- Value the people in your life.
- Don't get too attached to material things.
- And my personal favorite, "There's no shame in saying, 'I don't know.'"

Jesus said to Nicodemus, "I realize you're a teacher of Israel, but from the questions you're asking, I gather you don't know some important things that you really ought to know." (See John 3:10.)

Their discussion centered on how to be born again, which Jesus explained was being "born of water and the Spirit." If a person is not born again of water and Spirit, he or she cannot see the kingdom of God.

These Things You Ought to Know is meant to serve as a resource for believers in helping to establish their defense of the salvation plan, as well as a guide for serious searchers for truth. I wrote this book to help those who care about life; I want people to know what they ought to know!

Wisdom teaches if you reason with an arrogant cynic, you'll get slapped in the face. If you confront their bad behavior you will get a kick in the shins. So don't waste your time on scoffers. All you'll get for your pains is abuse. But if you correct those who care about life, that's different—they'll love you for it. Save your breath for the wise—they'll be wiser for it. Tell good people what they ought to know and they will profit from it. (Proverbs 9:7–9, MSG)

> "Sin" is a small word, but the act can lead to big consequences. The prophet Ezekiel proclaimed, "The soul that sinneth, it shall die" (Ezekiel 18:20). The apostle Paul said the same thing in the book of Romans: "The wages of sin is death." Death is not the end of existence; it is the state of existing without God, whether in this life or the next. People living in sin are described in Scripture as "dead in their trespasses."

We all are born in sin, and our attitudes, thoughts, and lifestyles are shaped by the sin all around us (Psalm 51:5). In this age of postmodernism, things have gotten so bad that people hardly know the difference between good and evil anymore (Isaiah 5:20).

Sin is an offense against God. It can be a sin of commission or a sin of omission. When someone commits a sin, they do something that the Word of God forbids; when someone ignores what the Word of God tells them to do, it is a sin of omission (James 4:17). At one time or another we all have fallen short; we all have gone our own way. With what result? (See Matthew 15:19; Romans 8:12; Jeremiah 17:9; and Genesis 6:5.) The person who lives a life of sin and does not receive God's plan of salvation will be sentenced to eternal suffering in the lake of fire. Eternity is a long time to be wrong.

Either God's Word means exactly what it says or it's just another book full of good sayings and fables. Some claim they don't understand it; others say they don't have time to study it; still others choose to ignore it—because if it's really true, it means they are required to make a change. Refusing to change means they love their sin more than they love God (John 3:19–21).

We cannot afford to ignore these things found in I Corinthians 6:9–10; John 8:34; Isaiah 59:1–2; and II Thessalonians 1:8. Make it your goal to know God and obey the gospel! Read Acts 2:37–40 and then do it.

Introduction

Oh that man would search the Scriptures and learn to love the excitement of discovery! It reminds me of the often-told saying, "Give a man a fish and you will feed him for one day. Teach him how to fish and you will feed him for a lifetime." How true that is concerning the Bible!

"Neither have I gone back from the commandment of his lips; I have esteemed the words of his mouth more than my necessary food" (Job 23:12). I regard the Word of God like a big juicy spiritual steak. A person shouldn't gobble it down, but they should take their time and savor the flavors. They should chew it slowly, tasting all of the spices and juices to get all it has to offer.

My love for God's Word began with being taught the home Bible study series titled "Exploring God's Word." Being taught while looking at the flip charts made the Word come alive to me. I could actually see what the teacher was saying. It ignited a hunger in me to discover more.

There is no book like the Holy book. It is a living book. God has spoken to me through His Word. He has given me personal instructions, interesting explorations, heart-pounding insights, and eternal precepts to teach and to preach to whoever will hear. Here in this book are a collection of sermons, thoughts, and gems of insights and scriptural wonderment that have blessed me through the years.

I credit it all to the Author and Finisher of my faith, the Lord Jesus Christ.

I read about a woman who was driving on the highway for the first time. Her husband called her on his cell phone and said, "Be careful, honey. It's just been reported on the radio that someone is driving the wrong way on highway such-and-such." She replied, "Someone? These idiots are in the hundreds!"

If, while reading this book, you discover you are going the wrong way, turn around!

Chapter One

Salvation God's Way

> The people of Berea were more open-minded than those in Thessalonica, and they listened eagerly to Paul's message. They searched the Scriptures day after day to see if Paul and Silas were teaching the truth.
>
> Acts 17:11, NLT

So many people today are biblically illiterate. Alarmingly, many of these attend church. I am shocked when I see so many in church services without their Bibles. Some simply depend on the leaders and teachers to do all the studying. They are not willing to search for themselves to see if what they are being taught is the truth.

I have heard many say, "I trust my pastor." "My bishop would never lie to me." "I was born a Baptist, raised a Baptist, and I will die a Baptist" (or whatever denomination). But what does the Scripture teach in relation to what you are being taught? I remember Bishop G. E. Patterson, a Pentecostal Holiness leader, singing this old song:

Chapter One

I told you once
I told you twice
You can't make it to Heaven
With a sweetheart and a wife

I know the Bible is right
Somebody's wrong
Somebody's wrong
Somebody's wrong!

Read the Bible
Through and through
It keeps on telling you
You've got work to do

I know the Bible is right
Somebody's wrong
Somebody's wrong
Somebody's wrong!

The Scriptures declare, "Let God be true, but every man a liar" (Romans 3:4). If somebody is doing something any other way than the Bible way, then that somebody is wrong!

That's why I believe it is important to answer these questions: How are we saved according to the Scriptures? What is salvation God's way? You may discover it is far removed from what you hear across many pulpits today. Some might say, "Lift up your hands and repeat after me" or "The doors of the church are opened." Others might say, "Just believe and be saved," or the popular phrase, "Accept the Lord as your personal Savior." These statements are unbiblical; they are examples of mainstream church tradition.

Let us consider the following Scripture passages:

1. *We must first **believe** in God*: "He that cometh to God must believe that he is" (Hebrews 11:6). "He that believeth…shall be saved; but he that believeth not shall be damned" (Mark 16:16).

2. *We are saved by **grace***: "Even when we were dead in sins, hath quickened us together with Christ, (by grace ye are saved;)" (Ephesians 2:5); "For the grace of God that bringeth salvation hath appeared to all men" (Titus 2:11). Grace in and of itself does not save us, but it "bringeth salvation." In other words, His goodness and grace lead us to His full salvation.

3. *We are saved by **faith***: "For by grace are ye saved through faith" (Ephesians 2:8). Grace is what God did to purchase our salvation, and faith is our response to what God did. "Without faith it is impossible to please him" (Hebrews 11:6); "Receiving the end of your faith, even the salvation of your souls" (I Peter 1:9).

4. *We are saved by **confession***: "With the mouth confession is made unto salvation" (Romans 10:10); "If we confess our sins, he is faithful and

just to forgive us our sins, and to cleanse us from all unrighteousness" (I John 1:9); "Confess your faults one to another, and pray one for another, that ye may be healed" (James 5:16); "He that covereth his sins shall not prosper: but whoso confesseth and forsaketh them shall have mercy" (Proverbs 28:13).

5. *We are saved by* **repentance**: "For godly sorrow worketh repentance to salvation" (II Corinthians 7:10); "I tell you, Nay: but, except ye repent, ye shall all likewise perish" (Luke 13:3); "The Lord is . . . not willing that any should perish, but that all should come to repentance" (II Peter 3:9). Repentance is a change of life and direction.

6. *We are saved by* **baptism**: "The like figure whereunto even baptism doth also now save us" (I Peter 3:21). We must never underestimate the importance of water baptism: "He that believeth and is baptized shall be saved" (Mark 16:16); "And he commanded them to be baptized in the name of the Lord" (Acts 10:48); "And that repentance and remission of sins should be preached in his name" (Luke 24:47); "Then Peter said unto them, Repent, and be baptized every one of you in the name of Jesus Christ for the remission of sins, and ye shall receive the gift of the Holy Ghost" (Acts 2:38); "Through his name whosoever believeth in him shall receive remission of sins" (Acts 10:43).

Salvation God's Way

7. *We are saved by the **Holy Ghost***: "Jesus answered, Truly, truly, I say to you, unless one is born of water and the Spirit he cannot enter into the kingdom of God" (John 3:5. ESV); "Now if any man have not the Spirit of Christ, he is none of his" (Romans 8:9); "For as many as are led by the Spirit of God, they are the sons of God" (Romans 8:14); "While Peter yet spake these words, the Holy Ghost fell on all them which heard the word. And they of the circumcision [the Jewish brothers] which believed were astonished, as many as came with Peter, because that on the Gentiles also was poured out the gift of the Holy Ghost. For they heard them speak with tongues, and magnify God" (Acts 10:44–46). How did the Jews who had accompanied Peter to Caesarea know without a doubt that the Gentiles had received the Holy Ghost in the same way they themselves had received it on the Day of Pentecost? The answer: "For they heard them speak with tongues."

8. *We are saved by **endurance*** (withstanding hardship/persevering): "He that endureth to the end shall be saved" (Matthew 10:22); "Blessed is the man that endureth temptation: for when he is tried, he shall receive the crown of life, which the Lord hath promised to them that love him" (James 1:12).

Yes, we must believe. Yes, we must have grace. Yes, we must have faith. Yes, we must confess. Yes, we must repent. Yes, we must be baptized. Yes, we must receive the Holy Ghost—the Spirit of Jesus.

Chapter One

And yes, we must endure to the end to be saved!

That answers the how-to-be-saved question, but now the question is what? What must I do to be saved? Fortunately, that same question was asked in Acts 2:37: "Men and brethren, what shall we do?"

Here is the answer:

> Then Peter said unto them, Repent, and be baptized every one of you in the name of Jesus Christ for the remission of sins, and ye shall receive the gift of the Holy Ghost.
>
> Acts 2:38

In this verse we discover the essential elements of faith, belief, repentance, the new birth of water and Spirit, baptism in the name of Jesus, remission of sins, and the inclusiveness of all nations.

Many pastors, teachers, and religious organizations have erred from the truth and have substituted a diluted message of salvation. You can read these verses for yourself. Search the Scriptures to see if you can find what these pastors, teachers, and religious organizations are telling you. They aren't there. But if the things I am telling you are documented in the Bible, then they are there for your example. Ask the question the people asked in Acts 2:37, receive the answer they received in Acts 2:38, and do what they did.

Follow the example of the Berean Bible students who examined everything the apostle Paul was telling them to see if it was true. With a world full of voices on every TV channel, in many pulpits, and countless denominations, all competing for your soul and telling you "this is the way to be saved," simply look in your Bible and see what the apostles have clearly told us in Acts 2:37–40.

There is no documented account in Scripture of anyone baptizing a person using the formula "in the name of the Father, and of the Son, and of the Holy Ghost." The Acts 2:38 message is the only documented plan of salvation given to the world by all of the apostles to make people like you and me ready for Heaven.

A lie doesn't become truth, wrong doesn't become right, and evil doesn't become good, just because it's accepted by a majority.

Don't follow the crowd, follow the Bible.

Something to Think About

Jesus taught that anyone who loves his life in this world will lose it, but anyone who dies to life in this world will find it. If anyone loves the things of the world—entertainment, money, music, or religion—more than the gospel of Jesus Christ, the love of the Father is not in him. Jesus said people can't serve two masters, for they must love one and hate the other. Some will try to tell you that you're saved just because you choose to believe. But belief alone will not save you. Salvation comes through believing the Word and obeying what it says.

Take heed to yourself; examine yourself to see if you really are in the faith. False teachings abound, and, admittedly, they do have a form of godliness. They may look right, but they deny the power of

God unto salvation.

To illustrate my point, I want to tell you the story of a man named Charles, who searched the Scriptures to see if I was telling him the truth.

Charles served as a devoted deacon in his church and enjoyed a legacy of ministers in his family going back many generations. It was just assumed that one day he would be a pastor in his family-run church. Very well versed in the popular Bible stories from his Sunday school classes, Charles attended my lunch-time Bible class at the shipyard where we both worked. He loved the lessons and gave a hearty amen to our discussions.

Besides Charles, there were many in my class from various church groups and denominations. I petitioned the Lord to help me to teach and show them a better way, the true way of salvation. The Lord gave me a three-point strategy: (1) win them to you, (2) win them to the Word, and (3) win them to Me.

After I had gained their confidence and taught them to consider God's Word as the final authority for all doctrine, I then led them to be obedient in their quest to follow Christ. I began to focus on the teachings of salvation.

At first Charles was very supportive, but I sensed some apprehension when I presented the question found in the book of Acts: "Men and brethren, what shall we do?" (Acts 2:37). It seemed he had been confronted with that question before only to become

Salvation God's Way

embroiled in a heated argument over who had the right answers.

I reminded the class that no man is right—only God's Word is true. In addition, the principle must be followed that a doctrinal truth is established in the mouth of two or three scriptural witnesses. Charles had progressed to the point that he trusted me, and he trusted the Word, but now he had to decide if he would trust God.

I encouraged the class to do their own research, rightly dividing the Word, citing the examples, and obeying any instructions given. Charles gathered his notes and list of Scripture passages from the lessons I had taught. He took everything to his pastor for clarification and discovered that his pastor's opinions contradicted the doctrine and practices of the early church. Furthermore, his pastor's explanations could not be validated by two or three scriptural witnesses. Charles prayed and studied, comparing verse by verse, passage by passage, and was alarmed at the lack of doctrinal teaching his church had to offer. He realized that what I had taught him was the truth.

But to accept this truth would mean that his salvation was more important than his tradition and his family legacy. He loved his pastor, his church, and his family's tradition, but he loved God more than these. For many days he agonized over what he should do.

Charles sat down with me after the next Bible class and told me that after searching the Scriptures, he had no choice but to acknowledge the truth with God's help and to shed the light of that truth to his church, family, and friends. Like the Berean believers, he "received the word with all readiness of mind," believed on the Lord

Chapter One

according to the Scriptures and was rebaptized—this time in the saving name of Jesus Christ. (Mark 16:16; John 7:38; Acts 10:48.)

Chapter Two

These Things You Ought To Know

There was a man of the Pharisees named Nicodemus, a ruler of the Jews, who came to Jesus by night, saying, "Rabbi, we know that you are a teacher come from God, for no one can do these signs that you do unless God is with him." Jesus responded to Nicodemus' question, but not in the way he expected.

> "Truly, truly, I say to you, unless one is born again he cannot see the kingdom of God." Nicodemus said to him, "How can a man be born when he is old? Can he enter a second time into his mother's womb and be born?" Jesus answered, "Truly, truly, I say to you, unless one is born of water and the Spirit, he cannot enter the kingdom of God. That which is born of the flesh is flesh, and that which is born of the Spirit is spirit. Do not marvel that I said to you, 'You must be born again.' The wind blows where it wishes, and you hear its sound, but you do not know where it comes from or where it goes. So it is with everyone who is born of the Spirit." Nicodemus said to him, "How can these things be?" Jesus answered

Chapter Two

him, "Are you the teacher of Israel and yet you do not understand these things?"

John 3:1–10, ESV

Nicodemus admitted that the same religious aristocracy that resisted Jesus' ministry also recognized there was something different about Him. Though they denied Him, they knew God was with Him because no one could do the things Jesus did without the anointing of God.

Nicodemus came to examine the Master for himself. The Lord looked past the religious relics of pompous titles, positions, and reputations and addressed the true deficiencies of the religious establishment. The fact was, though they were ever learning, they could not see the truth.

Not knowing is the same as not seeing. Jesus said, "I'm telling you the truth: unless you are born again, you cannot see the kingdom of God." (See John 3:3).

I can remember being in Mrs. Buckler's second grade class at Newsome Park Elementary School, sitting in the front row, unable to make out the chalked images on the blackboard. Other students didn't seem to have a problem, and I was too embarrassed to say anything. I had no idea if my vision was normal or not. That's when not knowing is the same as not seeing. I couldn't see what Mrs. Buckler was writing on the blackboard; therefore, I didn't know. It wasn't until a visit to the doctor for a childhood physical examination that my sight was examined and my problem discovered.

These Things You Ought To Know

I still didn't get glasses right away. I did fairly well without them, but as time went on, the strain on my vision got progressively worse. When I finally did get glasses, I remember being shocked at all I had been missing.

I meet people often who can't see the truth of the gospel. Some try to learn but never come to the knowledge of the truth, mostly because they refuse to obey the few small truths they have managed to hear. If you are not born again, you cannot see. Consequently, you become a victim of an enemy who will multiply your blindness and render you handicapped and unsaved.

> If the Good News we preach is hidden behind a veil, it is hidden only from people who are perishing. Satan, who is the god of this world, has blinded the minds of those who don't believe. They are unable to see the glorious light of the Good News. They don't understand this message about the glory of Christ, who is the exact likeness of God.
>
> II Corinthians 4:3–4, NLT

The minds of those who refuse to believe and obey are blinded by the enemy. If one refuses to be born again, he or she cannot see (cannot make sense of) the kingdom of God. It is like an expectant mother attempting to feed her unborn baby with a bottle by tapping the bottle on her belly. The child must first be born to get the bottle it needs to grow and be healthy.

Nicodemus, being yet unborn, leaning on his own logic and

human reasoning, was unable to comprehend. He asked, "How can a man be born when he is old? Can he enter the second time into his mother's womb, and be born?"

Jesus responded quite emphatically that the second birth is a spiritual event that involves water and Spirit. As it was in the first birth (the fleshly birth), it must happen again in the second birth (the spiritual birth). You must be born a second time as you were born the first: by water and by Spirit.

Born of the Water

While a baby is in the womb, it is situated within the amniotic sac, a bag formed of two membranes, the amnion, and the chorion. The fetus grows and develops inside this sac, surrounded by amniotic fluid. Initially, the fluid is comprised of water produced by the mother. Amniotic fluid also contains vital components, such as nutrients, hormones, and infection-fighting antibodies. Typically, at the beginning of or during labor the membranes will rupture— also known as the water breaking. (Lori Smith, BSN, MSN, CRNP, Medical News Today, June 27, 2018)

The word baptize is defined as being dipped, immersed, or surrounded by. In the first birth, the baby is baptized in the water that breaks at the onset of labor soon followed by the infant being delivered into new life. It therefore is born of the water. However, the birth is not complete without the next component. Here's an example of what I mean:

These Things You Ought To Know

I stood at the head of the bed in the delivery room with my video camera positioned over my shoulder. It was the old-fashioned kind of camera, and it looked like a Hollywood production was going on. My wife and I knew there was nothing like that first birth, and we wanted it all captured on film.

When Bethany was born, the attendants swiftly lifted her onto a table, announcing, "It's a girl!" I was so excited! I looked down at my wife and saw a look of concern on her face. She asked, "Is the baby all right?" I thought, Of course the baby is all right. But when I peeked over the doctor's shoulder, I thought perhaps I had come to that conclusion too soon. The infant was covered with gook and yucky stuff, and she didn't look normal. She looked like a lizard! "What's the matter with her?" I asked. The doctor smiled and said, "She's just fine, Michael. She will not always look like this."

I went over to Portia and assured her that Bethany was fine. However, a mother knows that everything is not all right until they hear that glorious sound. The baby had yet to take her first breath.

Born of the Spirit

The nursing attendants quickly took a blue suction cup and began to suction out the mucus from Bethany's nostrils and mouth. The doctor lifted her and popped her on her bottom. This caused her lungs to expand, and she took her first breath.

It is interesting that the word for "breath" in the Scriptures is the Greek word pnuema. Pneuma means "air in motion, breath, wind, or spirit." What do wind, breath, and spirit have in common? You cannot see them, but you can feel them and hear the sound they make.

> The wind bloweth where it listeth, and thou hearest the sound thereof, but canst not tell whence it cometh, and whither it goeth: so is every one that is born of the Spirit.
>
> John 3:8

That joyful sound—our baby's cry—was confirmation that all was well. Bethany was born of the water and of the spirit (breath), and along with that came the sound. Portia and I didn't know what the baby was saying, but it sure did sound good. Likewise is everyone that is born of the Spirit! There is a certain sound that comes with being born again of the Spirit. Hallelujah!

I must add the following unfortunate footnote to the story of Bethany's birth: I discovered later that in all of the excitement I had forgotten to hit the record button.

When talking with Nicodemus in John 3, Jesus was using a teaching technique He often employed by comparing a spiritual truth with a physical reality. A person once-born has physical life; a person twice-born has eternal life. Nicodemus, a very religious man and a ruler of the Jews, had trouble comprehending this simple truth. Jesus asked him, "Art thou a master of Israel, and knowest not these things?"

These Things You Ought To Know

The gospel Jesus preached—that of being born of the water and the Spirit—is the fundamental truth of salvation. This is something you ought to know. With no exceptions, you must be born again of the water and of the Spirit. How is this done? What must you do to be saved? I refer you to the scriptural passage where the question was asked:

> Now when they heard this, they were pricked in their heart, and said unto Peter and the rest of the apostles, Men and brethren, what shall we do? Then Peter said unto them, Repent, and be baptized every one of you in the name of Jesus Christ for the remission of sins, and ye shall receive the gift of the Holy Ghost.
>
> Acts 2:37–38

You may observe that I continually refer to the same verses. Why? Because the Scriptures are the foundation of all truth. They serve as our example, our guide, and our teacher.

> These things happened to them as examples for us. They were written down to warn us who live at the end of the age.
>
> I Corinthians 10:11, NLT

> Such things were written long ago to teach us. And the Scriptures give us hope and encouragement as we wait patiently for God's promises to be fulfilled.
>
> Romans 15:4, NLT

Chapter Two

Many people claim they are believers, but what they are believing and doing is not according to Scripture. Jesus taught that we must believe not according to our religious leaders, our parents, our friends, or television preachers, but, as Jesus said, we must "believe on [him] as the scripture hath said" (John 7:38).

Many religious people are wise and can understand certain things at an incredible depth, but if what they teach is not in accordance with the Scripture, then I consider them liars and God's Word as true. Those bold words are not mine; they are Paul's: "For what if some did not believe? shall their unbelief make the faith of God without effect? God forbid: yea, let God be true, but every man a liar" (Romans 3:3–4).

Something to Think About

There is a parable in the Bible about the woman who lost a coin in her house. (See Luke 15:8–10.) Is it possible to claim to be a Christian, attend church regularly, and still be lost in the house of God? Every individual owes it to themselves to examine themselves to see if they really are in the faith.

Jesus touched on this subject at the conclusion of the Sermon on the Mount, in which the Lord taught principles of Kingdom living and warned His followers about false teachers. He also warned them about one other thing: do not fool yourselves. (Note that He said, "Do not fool yourselves" rather than "Do not be fooled by someone else.")

These Things You Ought To Know

Not everyone who says to me, "Lord, Lord," will enter the kingdom of heaven, but the one who does the will of my Father who is in heaven. On that day many will say to me, "Lord, Lord, did we not prophecy in your name, and cast out demons in your name, and do many mighty works in your name?" And then will I declare to them, "I never knew you; depart from me, you workers of lawlessness."

Matthew 7:21–23, ESV

There are many who "say" but they don't "do." There are many who "know" but they don't "do." Too many people insist they are Christians, but they conduct their lives as if they don't believe the Bible. They refuse to submit to the ultimate Lordship of Jesus Christ. These folks generally fall into two groups: the casual and the involved.

The casual confess themselves to be saved because they "accepted the Lord at an early age." They don't go to church regularly; they don't have a prayer life; they don't understand the Bible; and they have no desire to change their ways.

Involved people call themselves saved because they play an instrument in the church or sing in the choir or throw themselves into the activities of the church. They know the Scriptures, know how to worship, and some even preach, yet they live with unrepented sin. They excuse themselves by saying, "Nobody is perfect," "God knows my heart," "Only God can judge me," and they try to balance out their sins by doing good deeds. These contrasts are worth thinking long and hard about.

Chapter Three
The Importance Of Doctrine

A s I besought thee to abide still at Ephesus, when I went into Macedonia, that thou mightest charge some that they teach no other doctrine" (I Timothy 1:3). The Apostolic Study Bible note on this verse says, "The key word 'doctrine' at the outset foreshadows [the word's] importance throughout the letter. The opposition faced by the church in Ephesus likely included both Gnostic and Judaizing elements. Here 'endless genealogies' falls in the category of Judaizers whereas 'fables' could be constituent of either [the Judaizers or Gnostics]."

Judaizers believed strongly that Gentiles must submit to and accept the beliefs and practices of Judaism in order to be saved. Many of these Judaizers followed Paul wherever he preached, stirring up strife, and even causing Paul bodily harm. The Apostolic Study Bible note on Acts 15:1–2 says,

Some Jews became believers in Jesus but held to the law of Moses, advocating that all males [including Gentiles] must undergo circumcision [the covenant sign given to Abraham] before being admitted into the church. Judaizers . . . were a persistent problem in the New Testament church.

As the gospel of Jesus continued to spread, the problem with Judaizers became more and more prevalent until a conference was called at Jerusalem. (See Acts 15 to discover the decisions of this conference.)

Gnosticism was another prevalent belief that the early church opposed. Gnostics believed the world was divided into two realms, physical and spiritual. They thought the created, material world (matter) was evil, and therefore in opposition to the world of the spirit, and that only the spirit was good. Gnosticism claimed hidden knowledge as the basis for salvation. Gnostics believed that secret revelation freed the "divine spark" within humans, allowing the human soul to return to the divine realm of light in which it belonged. Thus Gnostics tended to divide Christians into two categories with one group being carnal (inferior) and the other being spiritual (superior). Only the superior, divinely enlightened persons could comprehend the secret teachings and obtain true salvation.

These beliefs held by Judaizers and Gnostics were just two of the false doctrines that clashed with apostolic doctrine, and Paul and other early church leaders were embroiled in heated debates over these and other doctrines.

What is doctrine? Doctrine is defined as a creed, a dogma, or teaching; a belief or set of beliefs held and taught by a church. To understand the doctrine or beliefs of the apostolic church is essential. Consider the following exchange:

The Importance Of Doctrine

A man asked a church member, "What do you believe?"

The church member replied, "I believe what my church believes."

"Okay, then, what does your church believe?"

"My church believes what I believe."

Frustrated, the man asked, "Well what do you both believe?"

The church member said, "We both believe the same thing."

I contend that it's vital to know what we believe. Much is said about doctrine in the Scriptures, but very few people read or discuss what it is. What are those teachings that are so important that every believer should understand? Hebrews gives us the basic foundation:

> Therefore leaving the principles of the doctrine of Christ, let us go on unto perfection; not laying again the foundation of repentance from dead works, and of faith toward God, of the doctrine of baptisms, and of laying on of hands, and of resurrection of the dead, and of eternal judgment.
>
> Hebrews 6:1–2

This passage informs us there are at least seven foundational principles of the doctrine we should all know:
- Repentance
- Faith

- Water baptism
- Holy Spirit baptism
- Laying on of hands
- The resurrection of the dead
- Eternal judgment

Look at the instructions concerning doctrine:

> And they continued stedfastly in the apostles' doctrine and fellowship, and in breaking of bread, and in prayers.
>
> Acts 2:42

> Holding fast the faithful word as he hath been taught, that he may be able by sound doctrine both to exhort and to convince the gainsayers.
>
> Titus 1:9

> But speak thou the things which become sound doctrine.
>
> Titus 2:1

> [The NET Bible says, "But as for you, communicate the behavior that goes with sound teaching."]
>
> Titus 2:1

> Preach the word; be instant in season, out of season;

The Importance Of Doctrine

reprove, rebuke, exhort with all longsuffering and doctrine.

II Timothy 4:2

If any man teach otherwise, and consent not to wholesome words, even the words of our Lord Jesus Christ, and to the doctrine which is according to godliness; he is proud, knowing nothing, but doting about questions and strifes of words, whereof cometh envy, strife, railings, evil surmisings, perverse disputings of men of corrupt minds, and destitute of the truth.

I Timothy 6:3–5

For the time will come when they will not endure sound doctrine; but after their own lusts shall they heap to themselves teachers, having itching ears.

II Timothy 4:3

[Or, as The Message so aptly puts it, "You're going to find that there will be times when people will have no stomach for solid teaching, but will fill up on spiritual junk food—catchy opinions that tickle their fancy."]

We are to study the apostles' doctrine earnestly and continually, holding tightly to it until we ourselves can understand it and then teach it to others. Having a firm grasp on the doctrine or teachings of the church will enable us to recognize false doctrine. The time will come when some will turn from the truth and teach doctrines of devils. If you are ignorant of sound doctrine, you likely will believe anything.

Something to Think About

Blessed is the man that walketh not in the counsel of the ungodly, nor standeth in the way of sinners, nor sitteth in the seat of the scornful. But his delight is in the law of the LORD; and in his law doth he meditate day and night. And he shall be like a tree planted by the rivers of water, that bringeth forth his fruit in his season; his leaf also shall not wither; and whatsoever he doeth shall prosper. The ungodly are not so: but are like the chaff which the wind driveth away. Therefore the ungodly shall not stand in the judgment, nor sinners in the congregation of the righteous. For the LORD knoweth the way of the righteous: but the way of the ungodly shall perish.
Psalm 1

God is quite clear in His covenant with His people. He blesses obedience and judges disobedience. If you desire God's blessings, you must meet His conditions.

The people of God are called to be unique and separated from the world in our conduct, in our dress, and in our attitudes (John 17:11–17). We must beware of friendship with the world (James 4:4) that leads to being spotted by the world (James 1:27) and then to loving the world (I John 2:15–17). The result is being conformed

The Importance Of Doctrine

to the world (Romans 12:1–2), and, if we don't change, being condemned with the world (I Corinthians 11:32).

At first Lot only looked toward Sodom, but eventually he ended up living in Sodom. Spiritual decline doesn't happen overnight, but it happens gradually. The ungodly are people who are willfully and persistently evil. Sinners are those who miss the mark of God's standards and just don't care about it. The scornful are those who make light of the holy things of God (Proverbs 1:22). They laugh and mock at holy things like speaking in tongues, misusing Scripture to make jokes, and even mocking the Lord Jesus Christ. Several popular entertainers come to mind when I consider this. People have reached a very low level when they enjoy that kind of disrespect.

Chapter Four

Six Warnings From Hebrews

God wants the very best for us. He wants us to prosper even as our soul prospers: "Beloved, I wish above all things that thou mayest prosper and be in health, even as thy soul prospereth" (III John 2).

Yet there are some who find this way of holiness hard to accept. Jesus said in Matthew 13:21 (ESV), "Yet he has no root in himself, but endures for a while, and when tribulation or persecution arises on account of the word, immediately he falls away." Why is that? Maybe the question can be answered by the following example.

Some people are lactose intolerant; they have an allergy to the main carbohydrate (sugar) in milk. However, the problem is not with the milk but with the biochemical makeup of the person. The milk is good, but the person who drinks it has a hard time digesting it. In the same manner, there is nothing wrong with the Bible; it is the sincere milk of His Word. It's just that some people have a hard time digesting it.

Someone asked me, "Is it hard living for God?" I responded, "If you live for God easy, then it's hard. But if you live for God hard, then it's easy."

Chapter Four

If you love the law, you are free, but if you resist the law, you're subject to bondage. The police officer yells, "Stop in the name of the law! Keep your hands up where I can see them!" If the offender resists, the officer subdues him and whips out the handcuffs. Likewise, God says, "Surrender, and come out with your hands up!"

Salvation is a matter to be taken seriously. Thankfully, many pitfalls and problems can be avoided if a person heeds the following warnings from the book of Hebrews:

Warning # 1: Listen.

Listening is hard work. It involves our minds, bodies, and senses. It involves responding in obedience. "Therefore we ought to give the more earnest heed to the things which we have heard, lest at any time we should let them slip" (Hebrews 2:1).

We must listen carefully, intently, and purposefully to the truths we have heard, or we may drift away from them. Many things compete for our attention, even in a church service. When a baby cries or someone gets up and walks down the aisle or someone plays the tambourine off beat or someone is text messaging, we tend to focus on the distraction instead of focusing on worship and the Word.

> For if the word spoken by angels was stedfast, and every transgression and disobedience received a just recompense of reward; how shall we escape, if we neglect so great salvation; which at the first began to be spoken by the Lord, and was confirmed unto us by

Six Warnings From Hebrews

them that heard him.

Hebrews 2:2–3

If we are negligent in receiving this great salvation because we haven't been listening, we will not escape the judgment.

In addition, some hear the Word to no effect because it's not received deeply. "He also that received seed among the thorns is he that heareth the word; and the care of this world, and the deceitfulness of riches, choke the word, and he becometh unfruitful" (Matthew 13:22). J. C. Cole of Parkersburg, West Virginia, used to say rather emphatically, "The hearing is just as important as the preaching." The word is the seed, and when it gets into our hearing, it filters down into our hearts where it can take root in good ground and become fruitful.

But we must be careful to not just hear the Word, but also to obey the Word. James wrote:

> But be ye doers of the word, and not hearers only, deceiving your own selves. For if any be a hearer of the word, and not a doer, he is like unto a man beholding his natural face in a glass: for he beholdeth himself, and goeth his way, and straightway forgetteth what manner of man he was. But whoso looketh into the perfect law of liberty, and continueth therein, he being not a forgetful hearer, but a doer of the work, this man shall be blessed in his deed.
>
> James 1:22-25

Chapter Four

Warning # 2: Guard your heart.

Hardness of the heart begins when one refuses to obey the will of God. This leads to mistrust and unbelief in God. It's impossible to please God without faith.

> Wherefore (as the Holy Ghost saith, To day if ye will hear his voice, Harden not your hearts, as in the provocation, in the day of temptation in the wilderness: when your fathers tempted me, proved me, and saw my works forty years. Wherefore I was grieved with that generation, and said, They do alway err in their heart; and they have not known my ways. So I sware in my wrath, They shall not enter into my rest.) Take heed, brethren, lest there be in any of you an evil heart of unbelief, in departing from the living God. But exhort one another daily, while it is called To day; lest any of you be hardened through the deceitfulness of sin.
>
> Hebrews 3:7–13

A hardened heart is an evil heart of unbelief. Unbelief provokes God to anger. When you are challenged to make a decision, you have only two choices: either you will believe or you won't. There are no other alternatives. If you say, "I'll do it later; I'm not ready yet" or "I believe, but I'll wait for a more convenient time," you are actually saying no to God. And when you say no to God, you are really saying, "I don't believe you." And when you don't believe God and His Word, it is the same as calling Him a liar. That is pretty serious. You may not say it verbally, but actions speak louder than words.

Six Warnings From Hebrews

How long, O simple ones, will you love being simple? How long will scoffers delight in their scoffing and fools hate knowledge? If you turn at my reproof, behold, I will pour out my spirit to you; I will make my words known to you. Because I have called and you refused to listen, have stretched out my hand and no one has heeded, because you have ignored all my counsel and would have none of my reproof, I also will laugh at your calamity; I will mock when terror strikes you, when terror strikes you like a storm and your calamity comes like a whirlwind, when distress and anguish come upon you. Then they will call upon me, but I will not answer; they will seek me diligently but will not find me.

Proverbs 1:22–28, ESV

Each time you resist the Holy Spirit, your heart hardens until it becomes increasingly easier to turn away. The danger in that is God's Spirit will not always strive with man. There may come a time when God will grant you your desire to be left alone and then further harden your heart for you. Proverbs 28:13–14 says, "He that covereth his sins shall not prosper: but whoso confesseth and forsaketh them shall have mercy. Happy is the man that feareth alway: but he that hardeneth his heart shall fall into mischief."

Warning # 3: Grow up in the Spirit.

Lack of spiritual growth is spiritual retardation. In the natural world, a child cannot remain an innocent indefinitely; as the baby grows, he or she must train the mind, the senses, and the body to distinguish right from wrong.

For when for the time ye ought to be teachers [you old timers have been Christians a long time], ye have need that one teach you again which be the first principles of the oracles of God; and are become such as have need of milk, and not of strong meat. For every one that useth milk is unskilful in the word of righteousness: for he is a babe. But strong meat belongeth to them that are of full age, even those who by reason of use have their senses exercised to discern both good and evil.

Hebrews 5:12–14

Every believer should know the essential principles of salvation and be moving on to the deeper things of God. The writer of Hebrews said, "Therefore leaving the principles of the doctrine of Christ, let us go on unto perfection; not laying again the foundation of repentance from dead works, and of faith toward God, of the doctrine of baptisms, and of laying on of hands, and of resurrection of the dead, and of eternal judgment" (Hebrews 6:1–2).

Come on, little one, get up and walk. Try to talk, reach, grab, explore. Don't just sit there waiting to be fed; learn to feed yourself. Develop and grow in your own relationship with God. Exercise what you have learned.

Paul was pretty upset with the Corinthians when he wrote to them, "I... could not speak unto you as unto spiritual, but as unto carnal, even as unto babes in Christ. I have fed you with milk, and not with meat: for hitherto ye were not able to bear it, neither yet now are ye able. [In other words, you still can't eat meat! Why?] For ye are yet carnal" (I Corinthians 3:1–3). Paul had expected that by now the Corinthians would have grown into spiritual maturity. Instead, he had to admonish them, "For first of all, when ye come together in the church, I hear that there be divisions among you; and I partly believe it" (I Corinthians 11:18).

Paul was frustrated because the Corinthians were yet carnal. The definition of carnality is "to be fleshy, natural, worldly, unspiritual; given to temporary passions and appetites." "But the natural man receiveth not the things of the Spirit of God: for they are foolishness unto him: neither can he know them, because they are spiritually discerned" (I Corinthians 2:14). We have to exercise our spiritual senses. We must grow up spiritually.

Warning # 4: Have faith in the finished work of Christ.

To be saved, there is none other name but Jesus and no other way than by Jesus. Hebrews 10:19–21 states, "Having therefore, brethren, boldness to enter into the holiest by the blood of Jesus, by a new and living way, which he hath consecrated for us, through the veil, that is to say, his flesh; and having an high priest over the house of God." This is amazing! The shed blood of Jesus Christ provides a new way, a better way, to boldly enter into the presence of our holy High Priest. What a privilege!

The writer continued:

> Let us draw near with a true heart in full assurance of faith, having our hearts sprinkled from an evil conscience, and our bodies washed with pure water. Let us hold fast the profession of our faith without wavering; (for he is faithful that promised;) and let us consider one another to provoke unto love and to good works: not forsaking the

assembling of ourselves together, as the manner of some is; but exhorting one another: and so much the more, as ye see the day approaching.

Hebrews 10:22–25

Do not disregard what Jesus provided for us: "For if we sin wilfully after that we have received the knowledge of the truth, there remaineth no more sacrifice for sins, but a certain fearful looking for of judgment and fiery indignation, which shall devour the adversaries" (Hebrews 10:26–27).

We can't find salvation anyplace else—no other religion, no other savior, no other way—but at the cross and by the blood of Calvary. If we turn away from this, there will be no mercy.

He that despised Moses' law died without mercy under two or three witnesses: of how much sorer punishment, suppose ye, shall he be thought worthy, who hath trodden under foot the Son of God, and hath counted the blood of the covenant, wherewith he was sanctified, an unholy thing, and hath done despite unto the Spirit of grace? [You have understood the way of truth and rejected it.] For we know him that hath said, Vengeance belongeth unto me, I will recompense, saith the Lord. And again, The Lord shall judge his people. It is a fearful thing to fall into the hands of the living God.

Hebrews 10:28–31

Six Warnings From Hebrews

Warning # 5: Your life is an example to others. Make it a good one.

Hebrews 12:12–15 says: "Wherefore lift up the hands which hang down, and the feeble knees; and make straight paths for your feet, lest that which is lame be turned out of the way; but let it rather be healed. Follow peace with all men, and holiness, without which no man shall see the Lord: looking diligently lest any man fail of the grace of God; lest any root of bitterness springing up trouble you, and thereby many be defiled."

No one is an island unto themselves. What you do affects others. Your lack of passion, your depressed attitude and irritable disposition will cause others weaker than yourself to fall down and "turn out of the way." Look to the Word of God for direction and instruction in righteousness. Straighten yourself up and strive after holiness in your dress, conduct, and especially in your attitude. Let go of bitterness, self-pity, and vengefulness. Even if you feel the offending parties owe you an apology, forgive them their debts as God has forgiven yours. No one owes you anything. This kind of attitude will bring you peace.

Warning # 6: Only God's kingdom will last. Make sure you are part of it.

See that ye refuse not him that speaketh. For if they escaped not who refused him that spake on earth, much more shall not we escape, if we turn away from him that speaketh from heaven: whose voice then shook the earth: but now he hath promised, saying, Yet once more I shake not the earth only, but also heaven. And this word, Yet once more, signifieth the removing of those things that are shaken, as of things that are made, that those things which cannot be shaken may remain. Wherefore we receiving a kingdom which cannot be moved, let us have grace, whereby we may serve God acceptably with reverence and godly fear: for our God is a consuming fire.

Hebrews 12:25–29

See to it—make every effort to be certain—that you do not refuse the One who speaks from Heaven. There are a lot of voices, so many that it can be confusing at times. Therefore, choose to hear the Word of God because that's where faith develops. Jesus told us to search the Scriptures. In them are vast depths and heights, yet there are jewels of wisdom so evident a child can understand.

"The driver on the highway is safe, not when he reads the signs, but when he obeys them." – A. W. Tozer

Something to Think About

Here in a nutshell is the purpose of the book of Proverbs and its benefits:

Reading it and following its instruction will cause you to know and understand. It will help you to discern the difference between wise decisions and foolish ones. The more you "listen," the more you will learn. Keep these things you have learned close to your heart. To honor and respect your awesome God is the first step toward knowledge. Do not keep company with sinners and do wicked things with them. Do not walk with them, for their path will lead to nothing.

Six Warnings From Hebrews

Wisdom is crying out to you, "Don't turn away!" Some reject God's wisdom. They would rather be silly, argumentative, and foolish. If only they would turn to God, He would pour out His Spirit on them and cause them to understand His words. But since they refuse to listen when God is calling on them, He will not be there when they get ready to call on Him. But here is a promise: whoever listens to God will be safe and at peace.

Proverbs 1, paraphrased

"CHANGE WHAT YOU CAN CHANGE, TRUST GOD TO CHANGE WHAT YOU CAN'T."
-EVANGELIST MIKE EASTER

Chapter Five

The High Cost Of Walking Away

And when he was gone forth into the way, there came one running, and kneeled to him, and asked him, Good Master, what shall I do that I may inherit eternal life? And Jesus said unto him, Why callest thou me good? there is none good but one, that is, God. Thou knowest the commandments, Do not commit adultery, Do not kill, Do not steal, Do not bear false witness, Defraud not, Honour thy father and mother. And he answered and said unto him, Master, all these have I observed from my youth. Then Jesus beholding him loved him, and said unto him, One thing thou lackest: go thy way, sell whatsoever thou hast, and give to the poor, and thou shalt have treasure in heaven: and come, take up the cross, and follow me. And he was sad at that saying, and went away grieved: for he had great possessions. Mark 10:17–22

The Lord's ministry had caused an uproar in religious society. There had been many messiahs and prophets, but none compared to this Teacher. Captivated by His words, crowds thronged Him everywhere He went. His teaching stirred up great debates between those who held to the old traditions and those considered liberal in their views, yet neither side could easily dismiss this preacher from Nazareth. Religious rulers dogged His footsteps and scrutinized every word He spoke. They could not deny that His understanding of the Scripture was amazing. He did not speak as a student of the Law but as one who had supreme authority. Some of the scribes and religious leaders were in awe of Him; others feared Him and hated Him.

The Master ended His discourse and began to move away from the crowds to a place reserved for Him to eat and rest with His close-knit group of followers before journeying on to the next village. As He moved through the throng, He heard a voice shouting above the clamor: "Rabbi, wait!" The disciples looked back and saw a young man approaching. His fine clothes told them the man was wealthy and therefore ranked high in Jewish society. The disciples knew Jesus was not very popular in high-society circles, so it was unlikely this interruption would amount to anything but ridicule.

But the man repeated, "Please wait, Rabbi!" He finally pushed through the crowd to fall on his knees before the Master. The priests immediately recognized him as Adar, a member of the ruling class, and whispered among themselves, "What is he doing? Has he lost his mind? What's wrong with this younger generation?"

The crowd closed in behind Adar, curious to see what would happen. Adar said, "Good Master, what must I do to inherit eternal

The High Cost Of Walking Away

life?" A member of the religious sect holding an inscribed tablet asked, "What could he possibly mean by that? He's already saved; he's a minister, a ruler in the Temple. Why in the world would he ask what he needs to do to have eternal life? That is absurd."

But Jesus did not think the question was absurd. He studied the young man's face for a moment and asked, "Why do you call Me good? There is only one that is good, and that is God. Are you familiar with the holy commandments?" Heart racing, Adar looked up into the face of Jesus. He needed an answer, something to make this crucial act worthwhile. He hesitated a moment, then said. "Yes, Master. I have kept the commandments since I was a child."

Adar felt as if Jesus' eyes were piercing into his soul. What would the Master say? When the answer came, Adar was shocked and confused: "You are lacking one thing." Adar had just told the Master he had kept all of the commandments. What could be lacking?

The Bible does not ascribe a name to this rich young ruler, so for this account I chose to give him the name Adar, meaning "greatness" or "strength" or "mighty one." Jesus did not explain to Adar why He said there was one thing lacking, but it is obvious to me what He meant. Adar had called Him "Good Master." Since there is only One that is good, and that is God, then (in my opinion) Adar didn't see Jesus as God. It follows that, as Jesus said, Adar should not have called Him "good." So, correcting himself, Adar simply referred to Jesus the second time as "Master," leaving off the adjective "good." Though Adar was religious, the one thing he lacked was the revelation of who Jesus is. Just like the woman at the well, if Adar had known who it was he was speaking to, the conversation would have been radically different.

Jesus told Adar, "If you are to inherit eternal life, sell all of your lands and possessions, give the money to the poor, take up your cross, and follow Me. Then you will inherit treasures laid up for you in Heaven." Unfortunately for Adar, that was not the answer he wanted to hear.

There are many people like Adar who have grown up in church. The Bible has been part of their lives from their youth up. They've attended Sunday school and youth camps, they've sung in the choir, they've participated in many religious activities, and yet they remain in the dark as to who Jesus really is.

Great is the truth revealed concerning the Godhead, for God was made visible in the flesh of Jesus, proven to be God by His Spirit, preached among the unbelievers, witnessed by angels, believed on in the world and received up into the heavenlies. This revelation does not come by Bible studies taught by man alone, but by the Spirit of God. (See I Timothy 3:16; Matthew 16:16–17.)

In order to inherit eternal life, you must sell out. You must repent and believe the gospel. Repent, for the kingdom of God is at hand. Jesus said to preach repentance and remission of sins in His name.

Repentance is a selling out of the old lifestyle. The apostle Paul referred to it as dying to the world and the world dying to him. In other words, the world did not recognize, know, or love him and there was nothing in this world greater than his love for Jesus Christ.

You cannot serve two masters. It is impossible to love your possessions in this life and love God just as much. God accepts nothing less than a complete sell-out. You must be willing to lay down your life and pick up the cross.

Many people have difficulty making such a choice. But Paul said he counted everything in his past as "dung" compared to what he had in Christ. He gladly paid the price of losing all that he might gain all.

Sadly, there are too many that believe the cost is too high to follow the Lord, so they set their own standards or search for a more compromising choice. For them, taking up the cross is asking too much. They want an easy salvation with very little rules and no sacrifice. They consider true holiness as bondage; it's too strict and confining. It goes against the flesh. Yet without holiness, there are no guidelines and no boundaries. The outer areas are blurred, and the danger zones are hidden. They fail to consider that "without holiness, no man shall see the Lord" (Hebrews 12:14).

I am reminded of Earl, a friend from many years ago. Earl said to me, "Hey man, what's been happening? Haven't seen you in a while." Earl and I had grown up together in the same housing project. There was hardly a party in the neighborhood that Earl wasn't right there. He was a fun-loving guy, but every Sunday he went to church at 18th Street Mount Zion.

Chapter Five

I smiled big and said, "Oh, let me tell you. Things have been going great since I've been going to church. I am serious, brother; my life has been changed!"

Earl replied, "That's cool, man. I know exactly what you mean. Listen, Friday night they're giving Preston a birthday party at the Silver Dollar Club. You heard about it? You goin'?"

"No way, man. That's not me anymore. We've got a youth service at church. That's where I'll be."

"What church is that?"

"First Pentecostal Church on Culpepper Avenue."

"Pentecostal?" He did a double take: "Did you say Pentecostal?"

"Yea. It's the Pentecostal Church. What's wrong?"

Earl's eyebrows arched up and his eyes widened. "I'm just wonderin' if you know what you're gettin' into. My grandma was Pentecostal. They are holiness; those people don't play around."

"What are you gettin' at, man?"

Earl proceeded to educate me: "If you go to that Pentecostal church, you can't go to parties no more. You can't dance no more. You aren't sposed to get high or drink no more. I don't think you are ready for that!" He started shaking his head side to side. "I'm just tellin' you like it is. No more women! No more smoking! You won't be allowed to do nothin' no more!"

"Earl, Earl! Stop. I thought you would be happy for me, but all I'm getting is a list of all the things I can't do. Think about this for a minute. Everything you said I have to stop doing to be a member of my church, you're gonna have to stop doing in hell."

There was a long silence while Earl's countenance changed, scrunching up like a used bag of potato chips. At last, he said soberly, "What you sayin', man?"

"I'm saying that in hell you aren't gonna be goin' to parties. You aren't gonna be gettin' high with the boys. You aren't gonna be chasin' the girls or smoking. Well, on second thought, you might be smoking. But everything I have to give up to live holy for the Lord, you are going to give up in a devil's hell. So I figure, if it's gonna be given up anyway, might as well give it up living for Jesus."

For whosoever will save his life shall lose it; and whosoever will lose his life for my sake shall find it. (Matthew 16:25).

Please notice that Jesus did not bargain with the rich young man. The average church today would have fawned all over him. After all, he was rich and young, and he was on his knees asking about eternal life. Most pastors would say, "Why, come on in young man. Take your time. You will learn as you go." But, you see, Jesus was not interested in statistics and having a large group. He was not interested in the tithes this rich young man would give. Jesus Christ was more interested in quality of discipleship, and He never watered down His message. He lost a prospective convert when the young man turned away, but He didn't lose His message. We can't lower standards and compromise just to get people in the church. The truth is that some will stay, and, unfortunately, some will leave. Some will accept the truth, and some will reject it.

Salvation has a high price. Just lifting your hands and repeating someone else's prayers does not constitute the scriptural formula for salvation. Neither is living for God according to your feelings, opinions, or traditions. Many claim to have salvation, but their lives speak otherwise. You cannot get into the kingdom of God easily. It cost Jesus His life, and it will cost you yours. Jesus said, "If any man will come after me, let him deny himself, and take up his cross . . . and follow me" (Luke 9:23).

It will cost you your sins; you will have to give them up. It will cost you your pride; you must deny yourself, your will, and your way. It may cost you some friends, some of the old gang that you've been running around with. You may not drop them, but some of them may drop you.

Since you're reading this book, I want to tell you that you are facing the same choice as the rich young ruler. After you close this book to go on with your life, you will have to make the same decision. Are you willing to sell out and take up your cross this moment? Is it worth it to you to say, "By the grace of God, I will start to read my Bible and spend time in prayer. I will be faithful and loyal to the Lord. I will put Jesus Christ first. I will live a clean

The High Cost Of Walking Away

and holy life to please God. I will walk with Christ. I want Him to change my life. I want Him to forgive my sins. I want a new life, and with God's help, I will follow and serve Him."

The Lord said that whosoever would save his life (hold on to his old lifestyle) would lose everything, but whosoever would lose his life (give up his old lifestyle for the sake of the gospel) would discover new life. Abundant life. Eternal life.

It is the ultimate paradox: salvation is free, but it's going to cost you. You cannot do anything to merit salvation, but if you do nothing, you will surely forfeit it.

When the rich young ruler heard that he would need to sell everything and take up his cross, he walked away in great sorrow. The price was too high for he had great earthly possessions. He opted to have temporary satisfaction instead of eternal treasures. Yes, that should make anyone walk away sorrowfully.

Let's look at some good points in this story, along with one bad one:

1. The man came at the right time—while he was young.
2. He came with the right sense of urgency—he came running.
3. He came with the right attitude—he came kneeling.
4. He sought the right person—he came to the Lord
5. He asked the right question—what must I do?
6. He received the right answer—follow Me.
7. Then he did the wrong thing—he walked away.

Chapter Five

Don't be that guy. Don't walk away.

Something to Think About

Everyone will die someday, but will everyone go to Heaven? Practically every obituary tells of someone transitioning, being escorted by angels, passing peacefully into the arms of the Lord. Today most funerals are called home-going celebrations; in other words, a time to celebrate life. Songs like "I Can't Complain" and 'Let the Work I've Done Speak for Me" are sung with passion and conviction. The preacher tells the family that their loved one is in a better place with no more pain. We loved them but God loved them more. God makes no mistakes. The congregation is made aware that the deceased received the Lord at an early age and, even though they were not born again, they somehow made it into the kingdom of God.

Even some saved folks can't come to terms with the reality that a loved one has died lost. It is a painful reality, but to justify these feelings in the face of Scripture is a more painful reality.

That is why we must love God above all others, serve God above all others, and obey God above all others. It changes relationships. When Jesus was told that His family was looking for Him, He asked them a question and then answered thee same:

> "Who is my mother? and who are my brethren?"
> And he stretched forth his hand toward his disciples,
> and said, "Behold my mother and my brethren! For

The High Cost Of Walking Away

whosoever shall do the will of my Father which is in heaven, the same is my brother, and sister, and mother."

Matthew 12:48–50

It is appointed once for man to die and after that comes the judgment. Jesus died for us to save us from that judgment. "He who believes and is baptized will be saved" (Mark 16:16, NKJV). (See also John 3:1–6; Acts 2:37–41; Acts 4:12.)

Chapter Six
When Iron Floats

One day the group of prophets came to Elisha and told him, "As you can see, this place where we meet with you is too small. Let's go down to the Jordan River, where there are plenty of logs. There we can build a new place for us to meet."

"All right," he told them, "go ahead."

"Please come with us," someone suggested.

"I will," he said. So he went with them. When they arrived at the Jordan, they began cutting down trees. But as one of them was cutting a tree, his axe head fell into the river.

"Oh, sir!" he cried. "It was a borrowed axe!"

"Where did it fall?" the man of God asked. When he showed him the place, Elisha cut a stick and threw it into the water at that spot. Then the axe head floated to the surface. "Grab it," Elisha said. And the man reached out and grabbed it (II Kings 6:1–7, NLT).

Chapter Six

As the young prophet was enthusiastically wielding the axe, the iron axe head broke off of the wooden handle and spiraled into the swift-flowing waters of the Jordan River. The Jordan valley can range anywhere from fifty feet to two hundred feet deep, so the river is very deep in some areas. The chance of retrieving the axe head was obviously slim. Most tools during that time were made of bronze, so the iron axe head was valuable, which compounded the problem: the young prophet panicked because he had no money—he now owed a debt he could not repay.

We all have sinned and allowed our own heads to slip from the handle of the Lord only to fall off into perdition. We have been given the sentence of eternal death represented by the dark waters of the Jordan River. We cannot rescue ourselves. We cannot lift ourselves from the depths of sin and despair. We are hopelessly lost, for we cannot repay the debt that we owe for losing our place in God.

Romans 3:23 says, "For all have sinned, and come short of the glory of God." We are all sinners. We have all missed the mark. Romans 6:23 concludes, "For the wages of sin is death." The penalty for sin is everlasting punishment.

The apostle Paul summarized the problem when he wrote, "Remember that you were at that time separated from Christ, alienated from the commonwealth of Israel and strangers to the covenants of promise, having no hope and without God in the world" (Ephesians 2:12, ESV). Look again at the sinner's predicament: short of the mark, guilty, condemned, aliens, foreigners, and strangers. One day God will say, "I never knew you." You have no hope; you are

When Iron Floats

without God; you are without Christ!

Without Christ

The condition of the disobedient, unsaved, and those who refuse to believe is that they are without Christ! No tongue can tell the depth of wretchedness that lies in those two words. There is no poverty like it, no sorrow like it, and for those who die in that condition, there is no horror like that which awaits them in eternity.

In Ephesians 2:1–4, the apostle Paul showed us that without Christ we are dead in our trespasses and sins. We are walking according to the course of this world and according to the devil (the prince and power of the air, the spirit that is working in all those who are disobedient).

The unsaved are fulfilling the desires of the flesh and the mind, doing what they want and how they want to do it. By nature they are children of wrath. They are too proud to acknowledge their wretched condition. They don't see themselves as God sees them; they say to themselves, "I'm not such a bad person; I'm a good ole boy. I don't rob banks or steal from stores or molest children. Compared to those other people, I have a pretty good chance of making it to heaven." Their self-analysis is faulty, however. If they would see themselves as God sees them, they would understand they should be comparing themselves not to the standard of others but to God's standard—His holy Word. Then they would see they were desperately lacking.

So there they lay, like that fallen axe head, in the slimy mud of the riverbed. Dead in sin, covered by despair, drowning in hopelessness, weighed down so heavily they can do nothing but sink deeper and deeper. It looks as though they are lost forever.

But God...

> But God commendeth his love toward us, in that, while we were yet sinners, Christ died for us.
>
> Romans 5:8

> But as for you, ye thought evil against me; but God meant it unto good.
>
> Genesis 50:20

> But God will redeem my soul from the power of the grave: for he shall receive me.
>
> Psalm 49:15

> My flesh and my heart faileth: but God is the strength of my heart.
>
> Psalm 73:26

> Why doth this man thus speak blasphemies? Who can forgive sins but God only?
>
> Mark 2:7

> But God, who is rich in mercy, for his great love

When Iron Floats

wherewith he loved us, even when we were dead in sins, hath quickened us together with Christ, (by grace ye are saved;) and hath raised us up together.

Ephesians 2:4–6

...Raised us up!

What caused the iron axe head to float to the surface? Science tells us there is a buoyant force on any object immersed in fluid. If the buoyant force is greater than the object's weight, the object will rise to the surface and float. If the buoyant force is less than the object's weight, the object will sink. To put it flatly, iron does not float in water (or in most other liquids for that matter). Granted, objects with iron in them can float (such as most ships), but iron, as in a lump of, will not float in water. All of this tells us the iron axe head never should have floated—but it did on that day because God raised it up!

The prophet Elisha cut a stick and threw it in the water at the place where the axe head had plunged in, and, miraculously, "the iron did swim." In spite of Archimedes's rule of buoyancy, the iron axe head floated upward and broke through the surface of the water. I like to think that the wooden stick Elisha used represents the old rugged cross of Christ. To those who believe, the preaching

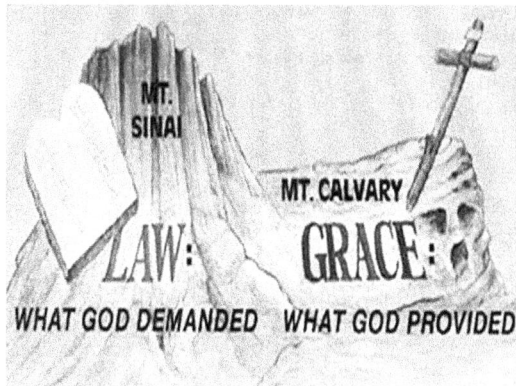

MT. SINAI / LAW: / WHAT GOD DEMANDED

MT. CALVARY / GRACE: / WHAT GOD PROVIDED

of the cross is a powerful, buoyant force that lifts sinners out of the miry pit. (See Romans 1:16.)

- The power of the Cross will lift the lost.
- The power of the Cross will lift the heavy weight of addiction.
- The power of the Cross will lift your sin-sick soul from the depths of the sea!

A man named James Rowe worked as a full-time writer, but he also composed hymns and edited music journals. His older friend, Howard E. Smith, had been an active musician throughout his life and served many years as a church organist, but by 1912 his hands were crippled by arthritis. Nevertheless, Rowe and Smith worked together, composing many hymns, one of which was "Love Lifted Me." James Rowe's daughter later wrote, "I can see them now, my father striding up and down humming a bar or two, and Howard E. playing it and jotting it down . . . The two huddled together, working line by line, bar by bar, composing this hymn in tandem." Here are some of the lyrics:

> *I was sinking deep in sin, far from the peaceful shore,*
> *Very deeply stained within sinking to rise no more.*
> *But the Master of the sea heard my despairing cry,*
> *From the waters lifted me.*
> *Now safe am I.*
>
> *Love lifted me! Love lifted me!*
> *When nothing else could help,*
> *Love lifted me.*

When Iron Floats

Love lifted me! Love lifted me!
When nothing else could help,
Love lifted me!

Souls in danger look above, Jesus completely saves.
He will lift you by His love out of the angry waves;
He's the Master of the sea, billows His will obey.
He your Savior wants to be. Be saved today.

Like the axe head that floated to the surface, God can raise us from the depths of sin into a new light, a new day, and eternal life. Like the young man who lost the axe head, we are unable to pay the price to buy back the salvation that we lost. No man has the ability to reach down and lift us up. It has to be done by the power of God through faith in the blood of Jesus Christ.

Call out to God right now. Allow Him to cast the cross of Calvary into the muddy waters of your life. If God can cause an iron axe head to swim to the surface of a swift-flowing river, He can surely lift you out of the mire in your pit of despair.

The man of God asked, "Where did the axe head fall?" The young prophet showed him the place. Elisha cut down a stick, threw it in, and the iron axe head floated to the surface. He told the young man, "Take it." So the man reached out and grabbed it.

The gift of God is eternal life through Jesus Christ. Why not reach out and take hold of it today?

Chapter Six

Something to Think About

Your salvation is based on your willingness to follow instructions. God's wisdom will give you discretion, which is the ability to see the truth and not be fooled. It will keep you and protect you from evil men. It will keep you and protect you from the strange or evil woman. All this is to guide you in the right paths that you may inherit the blessings of God and not fall into the trap of the wicked.

Proverbs 2, paraphrased

Wanda railed at her cousin, "I can tell you think you are hot stuff since you've been going to that church. But you're no better than anyone else. And tell your little prissy kids to stop telling my kids they need to get saved. My kids are already saved!" Wanda took another puff of her cigarette as she turned to walk away from her cousin Lexi.

Lexi had been in church only three months, but already she was feeling the heat from family members who thought she was going too far in her new religion. Lexi had truly been born again and wanted everyone, especially her family, to experience Jesus Christ in a real way. She had been excited to tell this truth to Wanda, her favorite cousin, but it was clear that Wanda had remained on the muddy downward path while Lexi had chosen to follow a cleaner, righteous path that led upward.

Lexi had made some bad choices in her young life. She had

When Iron Floats

been reckless and wild and wanted to get what she thought she deserved. After her third child was born, and facing the possibility of homelessness, she thought of the welfare of her children. She knew she was heading in the wrong direction and desperately wanted to change her ways. She started watching some religious programs on TV, and she prayed and asked the Lord to help her find a church.

It was during Thanksgiving week when a lady who lived across the hall from Lexi's apartment met her in the hallway and invited her to a small get-together with friends. Lexi was somewhat hesitant, but her loneliness prompted her to accept. She told herself, "It will only be for an hour, and there will be plenty of food I can share with my children. Besides, that lady is really nice and she goes to church regularly."

Lexi attended the small group meeting and met the ladies there, but she also encountered someone she had not expected to meet: the Lord Jesus Christ! For the first time, she felt His anointing and presence. It was Lexi's introduction to the apostolic faith.

After that, she attended every meeting, becoming a regular member of the group. It wasn't long before she began attending the church, where she repented of her sins and was born again according to the Scriptures. Lexi was gloriously filled with the Holy Ghost and walked in complete obedience to God's Word. What joy filled her heart and her world! Her attitude changed, her affections for worldly things changed, her life changed.

The more Lexi surrendered to the lordship of Jesus Christ, the more she learned to walk in wisdom and godly instruction. God was obviously blessing her life and her children. She began to see the world around her in a totally different way.

Wanda was not too excited about the new Lexi and set out to prove that it didn't make any difference how she lived her life. Her philosophy was, "What is going to happen will happen, and all anyone can do is hope for the best."

Years have passed since Wanda's heated dismissal of Lexi's faith. Wanda's little children have grown into young adulthood. Her daughters are young single moms, struggling with drugs and depression. Her son has quit school in hopes of being a rapper. He has fathered about four illegitimate children across town. Wanda has a drinking problem and is very sick.

Lexi looks at her cousin Wanda through eyes full of compassion and knows she is looking at herself—except for the grace of God. Lexi's grown son is in the ministry, and her two daughters are attending college.

Lexi and Wanda's stories illustrate that there are only two roads to choose in life, the broad road (Wanda's choice) and the narrow road (Lexi's choice); there are only two gates, the wide gate and the strait gate; there are only two courses of instruction, the wise course and the foolish course. Your life will be blessed if you choose the way of the wise.

Chapter Seven
I'm A Soul Man

Many people are more concerned about their body than they are about their soul. The body may live for several decades, but the soul lives on forever in either heaven or hell. In Scripture, the body is mentioned 154 times, but the soul is mentioned 473 times. That's about a one-third ratio. So what does that tell you about which one the Bible emphasizes the most—the body or the soul? The obvious conclusion is the soul.

You receive your soul at the moment of conception, along with the sin nature. (See Psalm 51:5.) Your soul is invisible and lives inside of your body. Think of a hand inside of a glove. You can't see the hand; you only see the glove. Take the hand out of the glove, and the glove becomes empty and lifeless, while outside the glove, the hand continues to move and live.

Your personality, thinking, affections, desires, and feelings all make up your soul. Genesis 2:7 says, "The LORD God formed man . . . and breathed into his nostrils the breath of life; and man became a living soul." First Corinthians 15:45 says, "The first man Adam was made a living soul." You have a body, your temporary dwelling place, the part of you we can see, but you are a soul, the spiritual part of you that we cannot see. Below you will find eight crucial things you need to know about your soul.

1. *Your soul is the real you.* Your soul is invisible and lives inside of your body. Your body is like a "motel" that your soul is temporarily staying in. On the day of your death, your soul will "check out" of that motel permanently. Like the lifeless, empty glove, your body will be buried while you will continue to exist in a spiritual state. You will continue to see, feel, talk, touch, hear, and remember.

2. *Your soul leaves your body at death.* "And it came to pass, as her [Rachel's] soul was in departing, (for she died) . . ." (Genesis 35:18). When the soul leaves the body, the body is lifeless and no longer feels or thinks. "The body without the spirit is dead" (James 2:26). There's a soul (spirit) inside of you just waiting to get out!

3. *Your soul cannot die.* "And fear not them which kill the body, but are not able to kill the soul: but rather fear him which is able to destroy both soul and body in hell" (Matthew 10:28). The NIV Study Bible note on Matthew 10:28 states, "Body and soul are closely related in this life but are separated at death and then reunited at the resurrection . . . [by] the One, God. He alone determines the final destiny of us all."

Luke 12:5 (NIV) states, "Fear him who, after your body has been killed, has authority to throw you into hell. Yes, I tell you,

I'm A Soul Man

fear him." The NIV Study Bible note on Luke 12:5 states, "Respect his [God's] authority, stand in awe of his majesty and trust in him. Verses 6–7 give the basis for trust": "Are not five sparrows sold for two pennies? Yet not one of them is forgotten by God. Indeed, the very hairs of your head are all numbered. Don't be afraid; you are worth more than many sparrows" (Luke 12:6–7, NIV).

4. Your soul is more valuable than anything the world can offer. It is so valuable that all the forces of good and evil are in a tug-of-war to gain it. "For what is a man profited, if he shall gain the whole world, and lose his own soul? or what shall a man give in exchange for his soul?" (Matthew 16:26).

5. Many people neglect their eternal soul for the temporary things of this world. "God said unto him [the unsaved rich man], Thou fool, this night thy soul shall be required of thee: then whose shall those things be, which thou hast provided?" (Luke 12:20). The rich man, thinking of his bodily comfort and fleshly desires, tore down his old barns because they were too small to store the bounty of his bumper crops. He wanted huge barns filled with produce and grains and all good things so he could sit back, take his ease, eat, drink, and be merry for years to come. His mistake was that he neglected to reap spiritual things for the benefit of his eternal soul.

In the parable, God said to this rich man, "You fool! You will die this very night. Then who will get everything you worked for?" Pouring all of his efforts and resources toward amassing temporal things had jeopardized his priceless soul.

6. We brought nothing into this world and we will surely take nothing out. Job's concern was the polar opposite of the rich man's concern. Job's focus was on God. Job had it all, but when all of it was taken away—his health and his goods, herds, flocks, camels, servants, even his precious children—Job's response was to fall on his knees and worship God. How could he do that? His focus was on eternal, not temporal things. He saw the hand of God in his tragedies, yet he praised God and did not charge Him foolishly. He said, "I came naked from my mother's womb, and I will be naked when I leave. The LORD gave me what I had, and the LORD has taken it away. Praise the name of the LORD!" (Job 1:21, NLT). In other words, "I had nothing when I got here, and I will leave with nothing [temporal, that is]." He declared, "But as for me, I know that my Redeemer lives, and he will stand upon the earth at last. And after my body has decayed, yet in my body I will see God!" (Job 19:25–26, NLT).

7. Your soul will live on forever in either heaven or in the lake of fire. Four hundred years before the birth of Christ, Socrates, the renowned Greek philosopher, drank poison hemlock and lay down to die. Realizing that his death was imminent, Socrates' friends asked, "Shall we live again?" The dying philosopher could only reply, "I hope so, but no man can know."

I beg to differ. According to the Bible, we can surely know. Those who are born again and believe in the name of Jesus Christ can be assured that they presently have eternal life (I John 5:12–13). The Lord said without doubt, whoever hears and believes His Word has eternal life (John 5:24). God is able to keep you and make you stand before Him in His glory without blame with great joy (Jude 24)! God is able to save those who draw near to Him through Jesus Christ (Hebrews 7:25)! Jesus clearly stated, "He who believes has eternal life" (John 6:47).

8. Your soul needs to be converted sometime during your earthly life. "The law of the LORD is perfect, converting the soul" (Psalm 19:7). The only way you can get to heaven is to be converted. This truth can be illustrated by the parable Jesus told about the rich man and the beggar Lazarus. (This is a different rich man than the one mentioned in point 5, and we don't know the name of either of them, so we will call this rich man Dives, the traditional name assigned to him. Dives simply means "rich man.")

Dives enjoyed a sumptuous lifestyle, feasting on gourmet food, wearing expensive clothes, and living in a lavish villa. There was only one annoying fly in the ointment of his life: the poor man, covered with sores, who sat at Dives' gate every day, begging for alms in order to survive. Every time Dives passed through the gate, he turned up his nose at the beggar Lazarus. Dives even heard him say a time or two, "Please. If I might have the crumbs that fall from your table, I would be grateful." The very sight and smell of the man turned Dives' stomach, so he always ignored him and went his way.

He was gratified one day to find that the odious beggar had died. Good riddance. Dives had no idea that during the night angels had carried Lazarus away to a place of comfort and peace sometimes called paradise.

Chapter Seven

Unfortunately, Dives died too, and they buried him with pomp and circumstance, marking the grave with a huge monument. The mourners had no idea that Dives had gone straight to hell, a place of anguish and torment. "The rich man also died, and [his body] was buried; and in hell he [his soul] lift up his eyes, being in torments" (Luke 16:22–23).

In that awful place, Dives looked up and somehow could see "Abraham afar off, and Lazarus in his bosom." Dives screamed, "Father Abraham, have mercy on me, and send Lazarus, that he may dip the tip of his finger in water, and cool my tongue; for I am tormented in this flame" (Luke 16:24). Abraham refused, reminding Dives, "Remember that thou in thy lifetime receivedst thy good things, and likewise Lazarus evil things; but now he is comforted, and thou art tormented" (v. 25).

Jesus warned people about hell more than any other person in the Bible. Since His words are true, we know that hell is a literal place. The Scripture reveals that hell is a temporary place where souls linger until the judgment day, after which an even worse fate awaits: the lake of fire, which is the second death. Then hell will be cast into the lake of fire along with Satan and his demons. There will be weeping and gnashing of teeth for eternity.

If you are saved, at death your soul will go to a place called paradise to be in the presence of the Lord. The apostle Paul said, "Whilst we [our souls] are at home in the body, we are absent from the Lord . . . and willing rather to be absent from the body, and to be present with the Lord [in paradise]" (II Corinthians 5:6, 8).

I'm A Soul Man

In Luke 12, Jesus spoke with Moses and Elijah, who will reappear on earth hundreds of years after their bodies lived and died and were buried. This shows that their souls are still alive. In I Samuel 28, the prophet Samuel's soul was alive and speaking from paradise years after his body had died.

Where will your soul spend eternity? You can know for sure.

> These things have I written unto you that believe on the name of the Son of God; that ye may know that ye have eternal life.
>
> I John 5:13

> He that heareth my word, and believeth on him that sent me, hath everlasting life, and shall not come into condemnation [hell]; but is passed from death unto life.
>
> John 5:24

The apostle Paul wrote, "For I . . . desire to depart [from this world], and to be with Christ; which is far better" (Philippians 1:23). In Acts 7:59, when Stephen was being stoned to death, he called upon God: "Lord Jesus, receive my spirit' [soul]." Stephen went straight to paradise. There is no changing our destiny after death. "He that is unjust, let him be unjust still: and he which is filthy, let him be filthy still: and he that is righteous, let him be righteous still: and he that is holy, let him be holy still" (Revelation 22:11).

Chapter Seven

Every one of us must carefully consider where we will spend eternity. Eternity is forever! It will never end. "It is appointed unto men once to die, but after this the judgment" (Hebrews 9:27). What will you do about your soul?

Something to Think About

A neighbor told me that he was not a spiritual man and was not interested in the Bible. The truth is that man is made of spirit, body, and soul. God first created the body, then breathed into it the breath of life (spirit), and at that point it became a living soul. The spirit (breath) is spiritual, the soul (the eternal nature of man) is spiritual, and the body (the flesh) is natural. So therefore, man is twice as spiritual as he is natural.

Your thoughts are very real, yet you cannot weigh them or measure them. Your memories can be vivid and clear. You can see them and even hear them but you cannot hold them in your hands and show them to anyone because it is from the soulish part of you. Even though there is no natural evidence, you are convinced that that part of you exists.

When the natural ceases to exist, the soul will continue for eternity. Where your soul will go in the hereafter depends on what you "go after" right here.

Chapter Eight
So What's Your Problem

Thou believest that there is one God; thou doest well:
the devils also believe, and tremble.

James 2:19

The devil is not an atheist; he believes without a doubt in the existence of God. The devil also is not a Trinitarian; he knows there is no such thing as a Trinity. The devil believes in ONE GOD, and that in itself is enough to make him tremble.

The word "Trinity" is not even in the Bible. The term "God the Son" is not in the Bible. The notion of three separate and distinct, coequal and co-eternal persons is not in the Bible. Yet three centuries after the birth of the early church, these theological terms became part of the Catholic dogma. It happened something like this:

The bishops at the Council of Nicaea (AD 325) chose the Greek word ousia ("being, substance") to indicate that the Son, Jesus Christ, is the same essence or substance as God the Father. They formulated the Nicene Creed, part of which appears below:

We believe in one God, the Father, the Almighty, maker of heaven and earth, and of all that is, seen and unseen. We believe in one Lord, Jesus Christ, the only Son of God, eternally begotten of the Father . . . true God from true God, begotten, not made, one in Being with the Father. Through him all things were made. For us men and for our salvation, he came down from heaven.

It wasn't until the First Council of Constantinople (AD 381) that a new "revelation" was inserted into the creed: We believe in the Holy Spirit, the Lord, the giver of life, who proceeds from the Father and the Son. The Trinity was finally complete. But wait! How can the creed say the Son is "eternally begotten," when Hebrews 1:5 says, "This day have I begotten thee?" And how did the Council figure that God the Father overshadowed Mary when Matthew 1:20 says, "For that which is conceived in her is of the Holy Ghost"? It just doesn't add up.

So are there three persons in heaven? I think not. Furthermore, there is not and never will be even one "person" in heaven.

What is a person? Merriam-Webster's Collegiate Dictionary defines a person as a "human being" or an "individual." I contend there are not nor will there ever be any human beings in heaven. "Now this I say, brethren, that flesh and blood cannot inherit the kingdom of God; neither doth corruption inherit incorruption" (I Corinthians 15:50).

So What's Your Problem

There's No God like Jehovah

The great Bible teacher and evangelist, Johnny James, gives this analogy:

> The one sun manifests itself in three principal rays: chemical rays, light rays, and heat rays. The chemical rays help us to study the sun; the light rays enable us to see the sun; and the heat rays make it possible for us to feel the sun. One sun, three types of rays.

Likewise, we know God by knowing the Father; we see God when we see the Son; we feel God when we are filled with the Holy Ghost. These three are one. One sun, the great light of the world; one God, the true light of the world!

- One God, three manifestations.
- One devil, three manifestations. He is the father of lies, the son of perdition, and the evil spirit—but no one ever says he is a triune devil.

There is only one God, and His name is Jesus. In his book, The Oneness of God, David K. Bernard states, "Jesus is everything that the Bible describes God to be. He has all the attributes, prerogatives, and characteristics of God Himself. To put it simply, everything that God is, Jesus is. Jesus is the one God. There is no better way to sum it all up than to say with the inspired apostle Paul, "For in him dwelleth all the fullness of the Godhead bodily. And ye are complete in him" (Colossians 1:9–10).

Chapter Eight

Jesus Is Jehovah

Bernard offers twelve verses of Scripture that prove Jesus is Jehovah—the one true God of the Old Testament. I will include only a few:

1. Isaiah prophesied in Isaiah 40:3 that a voice in the wilderness would cry, "Prepare ye the way of the LORD" (Jehovah); Matthew 3:3 says John the Baptist was the fulfillment of this prophecy. Of course, we know that John prepared the way of the Lord Jesus Christ. Since the name Jehovah was the sacred name for the one God, the Bible would not apply it to anyone other than the Holy One of Israel; here [in Matthew 3:3] it is applied to Jesus.

2. Isaiah prophesied that the glory of the LORD [Jehovah] would be revealed to all flesh (Isaiah 40:5). Since Jehovah said He would not give His glory to another (Isaiah 42:8; 48:11), we know He could only fulfill this prophecy by revealing Himself. Indeed, we find in the New Testament that Jesus had glory from the Father (John 1:14; 17:5). He is the Lord of glory (I Corinthians 2:8). When Jesus comes again, He will come in the glory of the Father (Matthew 16:27; Mark 8:38). Since Jesus has Jehovah's glory, He must be Jehovah.

3. The LORD said, "That unto me every knee shall bow, every tongue shall swear" (Isaiah 45:23). Paul quoted this verse of Scripture to prove that all shall stand before the judgment

seat of Christ (Romans 14:10–11). Paul also wrote, "That at the name of Jesus every knee should bow" (Philippians 2:10).

4. When Paul, the educated Jew, the Pharisee of Pharisees, the fanatic persecutor of Christianity, was stricken on the road to Damascus by a blinding light from God, he asked, "Who art thou, Lord?" As a Jew, he knew there was only one God and Lord, and he was asking, "Who are You, Jehovah?" The Lord answered, "I am Jesus" (Acts 9:5).

Robin Mark was inspired to write the song "Days of Elijah: There's No God Like Jehovah" (©1996 Song Solutions Daybreak). Here are some of the lyrics:

> *Behold He comes riding on the clouds,*
> *Shining like the sun at the trumpet's call,*
> *Lift your voice, it's the year of jubilee,*
> *And out of Zion's hill salvation comes.*
>
> *There's no God like Jehovah.*
> *There's no God like Jehovah!*
> *There's no God like Jehovah.*
> *There's no God like Jehovah!*

There Is Only One God, So What's Your Problem?

God is indivisible, incomparable, eternal, infinite, omnipresent, immutable, self-sufficient, almighty, and preeminent! He has no mother or father. No beginning and no end. Angels bow before Him, heaven and earth adore Him. He alone is God, the great I AM!

- "Thou shalt have no other gods before me" (Exodus 20:3).

- "Know therefore this day, and consider it in thine heart, that the LORD he is God in heaven above, and upon the earth beneath: there is none else" (Deuteronomy 4:39).

- "Hear, O Israel: The LORD our God is one LORD" (Deuteronomy 6:4).

- "Wherefore thou art great, O LORD God: for there is none like thee, neither is there any God beside thee, according to all that we have heard with our ears" (II Samuel 7:22).

- "Ye are my witnesses, saith the LORD, and my servant whom I have chosen: that ye may know and believe me, and understand that I am he: before me there was no God formed, neither shall there be after me" (Isaiah 43:10).

- "I, even I, am the LORD; and beside me there is no saviour" (Isaiah 43:11).

- "Thus saith the LORD the King of Israel, and his redeemer the LORD of hosts; I am the first, and I am the last; and beside me there is no God" (Isaiah 44:6).

- "But to us there is but one God, the Father, of whom

are all things, and we in him; and one Lord Jesus Christ, by whom are all things, and we by him" (I Corinthians 8:6).

- "God is one" (Galatians 3:20).

- "For there is one God" (I Timothy 2:5).

- "Thou believest that there is one God; thou doest well" (James 2:19).

- "To the only wise God our Saviour, be glory and majesty, dominion and power, both now and ever. Amen" (Jude 25).

- "I [Jesus Christ] am Alpha and Omega, the beginning and the ending, saith the Lord, which is, and which was, and which is to come, the Almighty" (Revelation 1:8).

Why Did God Say, "Let Us Make Man"?

Some may ask, "If God is one, and there is none beside Him, and He created the universe by Himself, then who was He speaking to in the Creation when He said, "Let us . . . "?

"And God said, Let us make man in our image, after our likeness" (Genesis 1:26). Yet God alone created man: "So God created man in his own image, in the image of God created he him; male and female created he them" (Genesis 1:27).

In Genesis 1:26–27, the Hebrew word for "God" is Elohim. The definition of Elohim is "out of one comes many." Some say that refers to many persons, or a plurality of persons that make up one God. I agree there is a plurality here, but not of persons. The plurality is one of attributes. Out of one God comes many attributes.

Let's examine some of these attributes of God that were involved in the Creation:

> In the beginning was the Word, and the Word was with God, and the Word was God. The same was in the beginning with God. All things were made by him; and without him was not anything made that was made. In him was life; and the life was the light of men.
>
> John 1:1–4

Who was with God in the beginning? The Word was with Him—yet John said the Word was God. In addition, He was life, and His life was the light of men.

Who is talking here? The Apostolic Study Bible note on John 1:1 states,

> John's Gospel begins with a theological prologue that introduces its central character by underscoring His diving origins, identity, and role in a new act of creation (John 1:14). The concept of logos (word) enjoyed wide currency in ancient wisdom literature and philosophical circles both before and after the composition of John. Proverbs 8, for example,

metaphorically personified the wisdom of God.... The primary meaning of ho logos (the word) in v. 1, however, must be derived from its correlation with the Creation narrative. . . . Logos can signify "reason," "communication," "utterance," "spoken word," "speech," "discourse," "articulated plan," or "self-expression." This Word was "with God" (pros ton theon) and "the Word was God" (theos en ho logos). . . . John does not, however, envision Jesus as a separate ontological person apart from the Father, a theological construct that developed in post-New Testament thought.

One God, Many Attributes

Proverbs 8:12 says, "I wisdom dwell with prudence, and find out knowledge of witty inventions." Here we have the voices of wisdom and prudence. Proverbs 8:14 says, "Counsel is mine, and sound wisdom: I am understanding; I have strength." Therefore, we can add counsel, understanding, and strength. It's starting to get crowded around here . . .

Proverbs 3:19–20 says, "The LORD by wisdom hath founded the earth; by understanding hath he established the heavens. By his knowledge the depths are broken up, and the clouds drop down the dew." In Proverbs 8, the writer personified wisdom:

The LORD possessed me in the beginning of his way, before his works of old. I was set up from everlasting, from the beginning, or ever the earth was. When there were no depths, I was brought forth; when there were no fountains abounding with water. Before the mountains were settled, before the hills was I brought forth: while as yet he had not made the earth, nor the fields, nor the highest part of the dust of the world. When he prepared the heavens, I was there: when he set a compass upon the face of the depth: when he established the clouds above: when he strengthened the fountains of the deep: when he gave to the sea his decree, that the waters should not pass his commandment: when he appointed the foundations of the earth: then I was by him, as one brought up with him: and I was daily his delight, rejoicing always before him.

Proverbs 8:22–30

The Apostolic Study Bible note on Proverbs 8:22–31 offers this insight:

Wisdom is an attribute of God, and as such was with Him from the very beginning, even before the dawn of creation. Some people use this passage in an attempt to make wisdom a second person in the Godhead. But the text personifies the attribute of wisdom as a woman in contrast to folly, as throughout this section of Proverbs. The Bible teaches the absolute oneness of God and excludes the concept of plural divine persons (Deuteronomy 6:4; Galatians. 3:20)....To say

So What's Your Problem

wisdom was 'brought forth' (vv. 24–25, 30) before creation also precludes any idea that it is a reference to a person in the Godhead. God is eternally existent; He was never brought forth.

Thus, in the act of creation God spoke to His many attributes: Word! Life! Light! Power! Knowledge! Strength! Understanding! Prudence! Wisdom! He declared, "LET US"!

When God created man, He created in him the same attributes: word, life, light, power, knowledge, strength, understanding, prudence, and wisdom. In His image, created He him. Alone created He them. Jeremiah 51:15 says, "He hath made the earth by his power, he hath established the world by his wisdom, and hath stretched out the heaven by his understanding."

In my opinion, if God were three separate but co-equal, co-eternal persons in the Trinity and therefore created man in that image, man would be born with DID (dissociative identity disorder or, as it is sometimes called, multiple personality disorder). I agree—that is a ridiculous notion.

God does not and never did need help or assistance. He does not and never did need counsel or advice. He does not and never did need anyone's approval. In the beginning, and all by Himself, God conceived, planned, and created the universe and mankind.

Chapter Eight

The Hymns of Early Apostolic Believers

"Although little is known of the man who composed the anthem 'All in Him,' early Apostolic antiquity reveals that in the first half of the twentieth century, George R. Farrow was a well-known minister and author writing several articles with strong doctrinal assertions" (Arthur L. Clanton and Charles E. Clanton, United We Stand). The Old Landmark ("Psalms and Hymns and Spiritual Songs: The Music of Early Oneness Believers," Archive for the George Farrow Category, March 6, 2009) states, "Perhaps the most well-known anthem of Oneness Pentecostalism is George Farrow's 'It's All in Him,' which so clearly delineates the inter-testamental Oneness revelation of Jesus Christ as the manifest Jehovah God":

> *The mighty God is Jesus.*
> *The Prince of Peace is He.*
> *The everlasting Father*
> *And the King eternally.*
> *Wonderful in wisdom.*
> *By whom all things were made.*
> *The fullness of the Godhead*
> *In Jesus is displayed.*
>
> *It's all in Him, It's all in Him*
> *The fullness of the Godhead is all in Him.*
> *It's all in Him, it's all in him.*
> *The Mighty God is Jesus and*
> *It's all in Him.*

So What's Your Problem

The Alpha and Omega,
The beginning and the end,
The Living Word incarnate,
And the helpless sinner's friend.
Our wisdom and perfection,
Our righteousness and pow'r,
All we need in Jesus
We can find this very hour.

"The hymns of early Apostolic believers were inspired by deep spirituality and the freshness of Bible revelations. They were… anointed and apologetic, glorifying Christ and intimating the deep truths of the Scriptures. The popularity of many of these hymns lasted throughout the early decades of the Oneness movement" (The Old Landmark).

Something to Think About

Proverbs 3 is full of great promises if we obey God's instructions. Here is the list of instructions from that chapter:

- Keep His Word in your heart.
- Don't neglect God's mercy and truth.
- Don't lean on your own understanding, but put your trust in God.
- Invite God to be involved in your decisions.
- Respect the Lord and stop doing what is wrong.
- Put God first in the offering of your tithes.
- Do not reject God's corrections in your life.

- Stay focused on God's Word.
- Do not let fear overcome you.
- Give to those in need as much as you are able.
- Do not strive or be angry with someone without reason.
- Don't admire villains and make them heroes.

Now look at the promises given to those who follow the instructions in Proverbs 3:

- Long life and peace will be added to you.
- You will find favor with God
- God will direct your paths.
- You will be physically and spiritually healthy.
- You will receive overflowing blessings.
- You will be blessed and happy.
- You will live safe and secure.
- The Lord will keep you from falling.
- Your home will be blessed.
- God will be gracious to the humble.

All of this is for the one who finds wisdom and gets understanding. To the one who digs for it, searches for it, studies it, and incorporates it into his or her life.

Chapter Nine

Which Way Is The Right Way

There is a way which seemeth right unto a man, but the end thereof are the ways of death.

Proverbs 14:12

I was a novice at driving great distances to preach revivals, but I considered it an adventure. I had been to the church in Lynchburg, Virginia, before, but this time I thought I would take the scenic Route 58, the less traveled approach. After driving about two hours, I knew I was approaching familiar territory as in the distance I saw the mountains beyond the Shenandoah Valley. I pulled into a service station and used a pay phone to call the pastor for directions.

"Hello, pastor, I'm not too far away. I have about an hour yet to get there. I'm coming in off of the interstate. What route should I take?"

Pastor Klinedinst said, "Get on Highway 460 and drive north. You will go through some small towns and will see some beautiful countryside. That highway will bring you straight into Lynchburg.

Chapter Nine

Now once you get to the city, look for a McDonald's on your left, then take a right turn at the traffic light. That road will merge onto a highway that will bring you to a T. Do not turn right, but turn left toward a school and continue across the railroad tracks. About one mile past the tracks, you will see a Kroger's sign. But just before you get to the Kroger store, you will take a right turn onto Old Forrest Road. The church will be on your left. You can't miss it."

"Okay, sir. I will be there early. See ya." That seemed simple enough. I listened to my gospel music and prayed for a great move of the Spirit in the services. The drive was refreshing and the scenery was breathtaking in the lowering light of the evening sun. It was dark by the time I saw the sign, "Lynchburg 3 miles."

"He said I should stay on this road and look for the McDonald's. Oh, there it is. Great. Right turn at the light. Good. This place looks so different at night. There's hardly any traffic. Now he said something about a T. Wonder how far I have to go to get to that?"

I checked the clock on the dash. Thirty-five minutes before service. I've made good time. Then it appeared—the intersection shaped like a T. Slowing down, I looked left to right. "Okay, he said to turn left—no right. Or was it left? He did mention both." Bright lights blazed from my rearview mirror as a car pulled in behind me. Feeling pressured to make a decision, I turned right onto a small two-lane country road that separated two large fields. The car behind me was seemingly insisting I go faster and get on about my business.

I kept searching for a school or some railroad tracks or a

Which Way Is the Right Way

Kroger's sign, but none of that appeared. As the road wound around a bend, I saw the lights of a service station, pulled in, and went inside, looking for a pay phone. I called the church, and the conversation went something like this:

"Hello, Pastor. I think I made a wrong turn."

"Okay, then, Brother Easter. Where are you?"

"I don't know."

"Well, where are you calling from?"

"Oh, it's a service station. Looks like a BP."

"Did it have an old beat-up green rusty truck outside by the road?"

"Yes, sir. That's right."

"Oh, Brother Easter, I know exactly where you are. You're not that far from the church. All you have to do is get back on the road and continue in the direction you were going. The road is going to curve to a highway. Go a bit until you see the place where you can make a U-turn. Turn around and go about four miles to Exit 4. That's the Forrest Road exit. This time of night you have to watch out for deer coming from that way, so be careful. Church is about to start. See you in a little bit."

Chapter Nine

I got back in my car, turned off the cassette player, and stopped praying, just so I could concentrate. The inky dark surroundings were made even darker by the huge mountainsides that appeared out of nowhere. Suddenly, there was the highway and then it turned onto an interstate. The signs were leading me away from Lynchburg and there were cars everywhere!

There was no place to turn around, and it took a while before I saw an exit ramp. I took that ramp and headed back in what I hoped was the right direction. All of the anointing I had been feeling on the way to Lynchburg was gone, replaced with anxiety. After what seemed like ten minutes, I saw the now-familiar "Welcome to Lynchburg" sign. I desperately needed to get to a phone. Driving now by instinct, I saw what looked like a roadside cafe. I went in to use the phone. The proprietor gave me a strange look as he pointed to the little phone booth by the restrooms. The following conversation ensued:

"Hey, Pastor."

"Brother, do you want to preach tonight? If not, I got a man here ready to go. Just say the word, doc."

"I'm trying to get there, sir."

"Well, where are you?"

"I don't know!"

Which Way Is the Right Way

"What building are you calling from?"

"Let's see . . . I'm at Billy Bob's Bar and Grill."

"Oh, my goodness! What're you doing at Billy Bob's? You need to get out of there! Well, don't worry. I know exactly where you are. Why, you are not that far from the church! Here's what you need to do. Get back on the road and . . ."

"Wait! Please listen, Pastor. You know where I am, but I don't know where you are. How about if you send somebody—anybody—to meet me here. I will gladly follow anyone who knows which way is the right way!"

Isn't that how you feel sometimes? You just want to follow someone who knows which way is the right way. Have you ever wondered why there are so many denominations under the banner of Christianity? Are there really that many ways to be saved?

The word "denomination" is a financial term. When one walks up to a bank teller, pulls out a bill, and asks the teller to break it down into smaller bills, the teller may ask, "What denominations would you like?" In other words, "How would you like this bill divided?" Well, the body of Christ is not divided. In his first letter to the Corinthian church, the apostle Paul stated,

> Now I beseech you, brethren, by the name of our
> Lord Jesus Christ, that ye all speak the same thing,
> and that there be no divisions among you; but that ye

be perfectly joined together in the same mind and in the same judgment. For it hath been declared unto me of you, my brethren, by them which are of the house of Chloe, that there are contentions among you. Now this I say, that every one of you saith, I am of Paul; and I of Apollos; and I of Cephas; and I of Christ. Is Christ divided? was Paul crucified for you? or were ye baptized in the name of Paul?

I Corinthians 1:10–13

Of course, the answer to those three questions is no.

Later on in the letter, Paul stated, "For just as the body is one and has many members, and all members of the body, though many, are one body, so it is with Christ" (I Corinthians 12:12, ESV). The body of Christ is not a denomination nor is it several different beliefs. Jesus said, "Upon this rock I will build My church." He did not say, "I will build My churches."

One Lord

There is only "one Lord" (Ephesians 4:5). Make sure you believe in Him. Jesus is the head of the church—not a priest, a pope, or a TV preacher. There is only one "head," and that is the Lord Jesus Christ.

"Jesus saith unto them, Did ye never read in the scriptures, The stone which the builders rejected, the same is become the head of the corner: this is the Lord's doing, and it is marvellous in our eyes?" (Matthew 21:42). (See also Mark 12:10; Luke 20:17.)

Which Way Is the Right Way

He wrought [this] in Christ, when he raised him from
the dead, and set him at his own right hand [not a
special position, but one of power and authority] in
the heavenly places, far above all principality, and
power, and might, and dominion, and every name
that is named, not only in this world, but also in that
which is to come: and hath put all things under his
feet, and gave him to be the head over all things to
the church, which is his body, the fullness of him that
filleth all in all.

Ephesians 1:20–23

The Apostolic Study Bible note on Ephesians 1:23 states,

The church, as Christ's body, comprises the fullness
of Christ, who is in the process of filling the universe
in every respect. . . . While Christ is in the process of
filling the world with His absolute rule, in this age only
the church is 'filled' with Christ and in submission to
his total sway. And while all spiritual powers may
(resentfully) acknowledge Christ's authority (Acts
19:15), only the church gratefully welcomes His
authority. As the church grows, the rule of Christ
grows. As the church spreads, the spiritual powers
that oppress people begin to diminish—and Christ's
dominion spreads.

[That you might] grow up into him in all things, which is the head, even Christ.

Ephesians 4:15

Christ is the head of the church: and he is the saviour of the body.

Ephesians 5:23

And he [Christ] is the head of the body, the church: who is the beginning, the firstborn from the dead; that in all things he might have the preeminence.

Colossians 1:18

And ye are complete in him, which is the head of all principality and power.

Colossians 2:10

One Faith

There is only one faith (Ephesians 4:5).

Catholic faith? Baptist faith? Jehovah's Witnesses faith? Methodist faith? Presbyterian faith? Islamic faith? Buddhist faith? Hindu faith? I could go on and on, but what's the point? There is only one faith acceptable to God. And we are instructed to contend or fight for that particular faith that was delivered by Christ to the apostles.

Which Way Is the Right Way

> Beloved, when I gave all diligence to write unto you of the common salvation, it was needful for me to write unto you, and exhort you that ye should earnestly contend for the faith which was once delivered unto the saints.

Jude 3

Search, strive, and fight for the same faith, the same doctrine and teachings of the saints of God in the Scripture. Believe what John believed; preach what Paul preached; do what Peter commanded. There is only one faith. Make sure you are in it.

One Baptism

There is only one baptism (Ephesians 4:5). Make sure you submit to it.

The Lord commanded this water baptism for everybody in all nations. He said it was to be administered in the name of the Father, and of the Son, and of the Holy Ghost, and in His name for the remission of sins (Matthew 28:19; Luke 24:47). There is only one name in water baptism whereby we all must be saved (Acts 4:12). He instructed that this gospel was to be preached first in Jerusalem, then in Samaria, and then in the uttermost parts of the world. Throughout the book of Acts, we see the fulfillment of this command and the correct way to be baptized. Search the Scriptures: Mark 16:15–16; Romans 6:3–7; Acts 2:38; 8:12–17; 10:48; 19:1–6; Galatians 3:26–28.

Chapter Nine

If I were to ask you to write out a check payable in the name of your father, what name would you use? Would you sign it like this: "in the name of my father"? Or would you actually use his name? Would it make a difference?

- What is the name of the Father? Jesus said, "I am come in my Father's name (John 5:43).
- What is the name of the Son? Matthew stated the name in large, bold letters: JESUS (Matthew 1:21).
- What is the name of the Holy Ghost? Jesus said the Comforter is the "Holy Ghost, whom the Father will send in my name" (John 14:26).

The name does make a difference!

- "Salvation is found in no one else, for there is no other name under heaven given to mankind by which we must be saved" (Acts 4:12, NIV).
- "And whatsoever ye do in word or deed, do all in the name of the Lord Jesus, giving thanks to God and the Father by him" (Colossians 3:17).

You can do the right thing the wrong way. For instance, it was right that the children of Israel wanted to praise the Lord, but they did it the wrong way by making an idol of gold. It was right that David returned the Ark to Jerusalem, but the Ark was in a cart instead of being borne on the shoulders of the priests. He did the right thing the wrong way.

Which Way Is the Right Way

At Rephidim, in the Wilderness of Sinai, the need for water for millions of people and animals must have been an immense problem. There would have been no sin in asking Moses for water, but the Bible says the Israelites "contended" or "chided" with Moses. In Exodus 17:2, this verb means "grumpy complaining." The Nelson Study Bible note on Exodus 17:2 states, "Moses judged this to be a challenge to God's faithful mercy, and evidence of unbelief in His provision. This was not the first time that the people had railed against Moses ... sadly, it would not be the last." God told Moses that He would stand before him on the rock in Horeb, and Moses should strike the rock. When he did, abundant water gushed out of the rock. Moses did the right thing.

The second incident, however, did not turn out so well. Several years after the first incident, the children of Israel arrived at Kadesh for a second time. They had camped there before without any mention of a water shortage, but this second time was different. This time, instead of telling Moses to strike the rock, God told him to speak to the rock in the sight of all the people, and water would gush out of the rock.

We have no way of knowing exactly what was going through Moses' mind when he picked up the rod. That rod had been with him during his shepherd days, during the plagues in Egypt, during the crossing of the Red Sea, and during the years of wilderness wandering. All of those times he had done exactly what God said. But this time was different. The dissatisfied, rebellious rumblings of the congregation had stretched Moses to the breaking point. In a rage and in the sight of all Israel, he struck the rock not once—as he had before—but twice. Still, God was faithful, and water once again gushed out of the rock, but Moses' disobedience cost him his place in the Promised Land. This time he did the wrong thing.

It was right that you were baptized, but did you do it the wrong way? There are many ways that seem right, feel right, and look right. But the question you must answer is, is it right?

Something to Think About

The Analogy of Two Women in Proverbs 9

Sometimes I watch the masses of people busily scurrying about like ants on an anthill, running to and fro, seemingly with no idea of where they are headed. I pray they will end up at the right house.

I hear a voice that rings true in the midst of the confusion: "Come to me! Enter into the house of the Lord!" This wise woman sends out messengers calling to the simple and those searching for understanding to come in and find life, blessing, and benefits. "Forsake foolishness and live! Fear the Lord and you will become wise, for the knowledge of the holy is understanding." The wise woman "has done her part; now the feckless and senseless must make a decision to feast and be healed" (Bruce K. Waltke, The Book of Proverbs). (Read the proverb of Jesus in Luke 14:15–24 about inviting people to a feast.)

But wait! There is a much louder voice, speaking great swelling words. It is a sly, foolish woman sitting in front of her house and

Which Way Is the Right Way

calling to the simple and those searching for understanding: "Come in, come in! It is far better in my house!" When they are drawn in, she seduces them with the pleasures of sin. She tells them no one needs to know they've been with her. But the secret in her house is death, and her guests are in the depths of hell.

These two women represent true and false religion.

The church of the New Testament is still the true church today and will be until Jesus comes. What Jesus taught, the apostles confirmed (Hebrews 2:3). The New Testament church continued in the apostles' doctrine (Acts 2:41–42). The doctrine is the standards and teachings given to the church by the apostles. The right church teaches the same thing today.

When discussing the subject of salvation, I always start at the beginning. If a church teaches anything different on this subject than what the apostles taught, nothing else they do really matters. And it is amazing how many churches teach a different doctrine than the apostles' doctrine.

A person can be very religious and still not be saved. For example, Nicodemus was a ruler in Israel, but Jesus told him he needed to be born again of water and of the Spirit (John 3:1–5) or he would never even see the kingdom of God.

The book of Acts shows us what needs to be done concerning salvation. It shows us what is commanded of God. Read Acts 10:1–48. This chapter highlights the salvation experience of a man named

Cornelius, who was devout, feared God, gave alms, and prayed. Yet he still was not saved. We know this because God sent an angel to Cornelius, telling him to send for a man named Peter, who would tell him what he ought to do to be saved. When Peter arrived at Cornelius's house and began to preach, the Holy Ghost fell on Cornelius's friends and family. Then "… he [Peter] commanded them to be baptized in the name of the Lord…" (Acts 10:48). The Holy Ghost filled the people and they were water baptized (Acts 10:44–48).

In Acts 19, the apostle Paul passed through the upper coasts and came to the city of Ephesus where he found "certain disciples." The group included about twelve men, and there could have been women there as well. These people had already believed and been baptized, but when they heard Paul preach, they found out they weren't baptized according to the apostles' teaching, so they submitted to baptism in the name of the Lord Jesus (Acts 19:1–7).

On the Day of Pentecost, when the church was first started, it was the same way. About three thousand souls "gladly received his [Peter's] word and were baptized" (Acts 2:41). The word Peter had preached to them was "Repent, and be baptized every one of you in the name of Jesus Christ for the remission of sins, and ye shall receive the gift of the Holy Ghost" (Acts 2:38).

The true church, the right church, baptizes people the same way today.

All churches are not the same, and all don't preach salvation the

Which Way Is the Right Way

same. If you are considering a church, ask them how they baptize and compare it to what the apostles did and taught. Follow the teachings of the apostles and you will be saved.

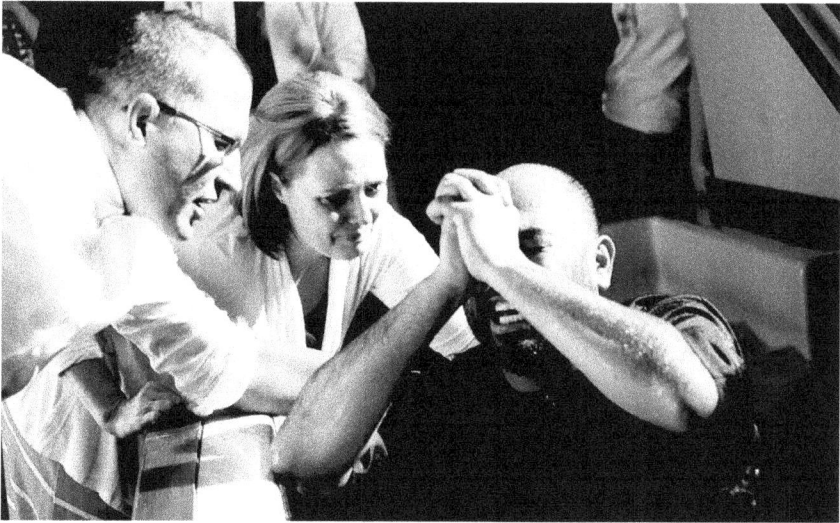

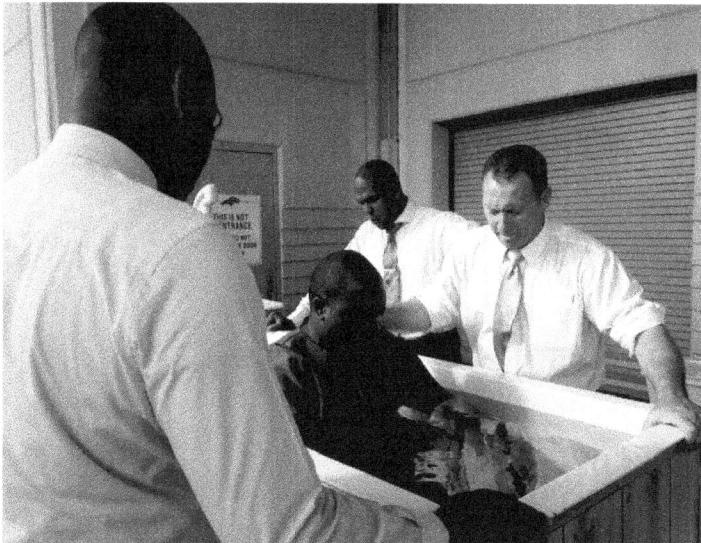

Chapter Ten

Jesus Made The Choice

Ye have not chosen me, but I have chosen you, and
ordained you, that ye should go and bring forth fruit,
and that your fruit should remain: that whatsoever
ye shall ask of the Father in my name, he may give
it you.

John 15:16

It's a wonderful feeling to be chosen, to consider that out of the
billions of people on the planet, the Almighty God chose me. I
can relate to the psalmist David when he wrote, "When I consider
the work of Your hands and all of the great things You have done,
who am I that You are mindful of me?"

Growing up, I was a short, skinny little guy. I had no brothers,
and I envied the boys across the street; theirs was a family of six
brothers. They were a rough bunch and knew how to punch and
take a punch. I guess they had a lot of practice. Of course, I wasn't
allowed to hit my sisters, so I didn't gain much fighting experience
there.

Chapter Ten

I enjoyed sports but didn't get much experience playing either. I just wasn't tough enough. I had little stamina and was uncoordinated. I did more scorekeeping than participating. I remember one day in high school gym class when the coach divided the boys into two groups for a game of tag football. The jocks were to choose their teams. The tall, muscular fifteen-year-old said, "I go first! Give me Calvin." Calvin was faster than greased lightning.

The other boy said, "Okay then, I'll take Larry." His brother played on the high school team. One by one they chose their teammates:

"Peanut, you're on my side."

"All right then, give me Bubba." Bubba wasn't very bright, but he was huge and had just got out of reform school. No one would dare try to tackle him.

Finally the captains clapped their hands and said, "Okay, let's do it." They ran to their places on the field and there I was, alone and not knowing which way to go. So I ran over to one team and they all shouted, "You belong over there! You're on the other team!"

I thought, I must have missed them calling my name. Great. But when I skipped over to the other side, they said, "You must be on their team. Nobody over here chose you."

My gym teacher shook his head and told me to just pick a team. By that time, I really didn't want to play anymore. I just wanted to

Jesus Made The Choice

get away somewhere and read my comic books.

That wasn't the worst thing, though. As I got older, my voice didn't mature until I was about eighteen, and I didn't grow much taller than I had been at thirteen or fourteen. So acquiring a girlfriend was a challenge. Girls would say, "You're a nice guy, Michael-Easter [they always ran my whole name together], but I just like you as a friend" or "You're too short." Comments like that would deflate me.

Then it happened. In my early thirties and after six years in the church, a little girl from West Virginia saw something in me that she couldn't resist. (Don't tell her I said that.) I'll never forget the evening I timidly proposed to her. I had memorized some lyrics from a love song and was ready to blow her mind, but I heard myself stuttering, "Y-you wouldn't want to m-marry me would you?" To which she answered, "Let me get back with you. I will have to think about it." I was more than a little worried. I thought maybe I would become a Pentecostal priest. She took her sweet time but finally said yes. What a thrill to be wanted! What a joy to have someone choose me!

How humbling it is to consider that as much as we needed Jesus, it was not we who chose Him. Though our needs were many, our hearts were so hard that we chose just about everything else but Him. We were so dead in our sins that we couldn't possibly have chosen Him. But while we were yet sinners, Christ died for our sins, and while we were yet running away from Him, Christ made His choice. He chose us!

Chapter Ten

God chose Abel over Cain, Joseph and David over their brothers, and Jacob over Esau. The apostle Paul was quoting Malachi 1:2–3 when he wrote, "As it is written, Jacob have I loved, but Esau have I hated. What shall we say then? Is there unrighteousness with God? God forbid. For he saith to Moses, I will have mercy on whom I will have mercy, and I will have compassion on whom I will have compassion" (Romans 9:13–15). The contrast of "Jacob have I loved, but Esau have I hated" does not mean God detested Esau or harbored personal animosity against him. It was simply "an idiomatic expression indicating . . . preference and means, 'I have chosen Jacob instead of Esau'" (Apostolic Study Bible note on Romans 9:13). It was simply God's choice.

> Ye are my witnesses, saith the LORD, and my servant
> whom I have chosen: that ye may know and believe
> me, and understand that I am he: before me there was
> no God formed, neither shall there be after me.
>
> Isaiah 43:10

No man can come to the Father except God draws Him. That's why when you feel that prompting in your heart to draw close to God, or that feeling that you need God, you must respond because it's God who is causing you to feel that way. God is drawing you to Him.

Man does not naturally choose God. His natural ears are so deaf they cannot hear His voice; man's natural eyes are so blind they cannot see the way. And the devil is bound and determined to keep it that way: "In whom the god of this world hath blinded the minds of them which believe not, lest the light of the glorious gospel of Christ, who is the image of God, should shine unto them" (II Corinthians 4:4).

Man cannot choose God because he is spiritually dead. He feels no attraction to spiritual things; they are foolishness to him. He sees no beauty in the Savior, no glory in the cross. Jesus came to save man from the thing he loves. Man finds it difficult to choose God because he loves his pleasures too much.

Jesus shed His blood and ransomed His life on the cross for you. Have you chosen Him? He has provided instruction and guidance for you through His written Word, the Bible. Have you chosen Him? He has blessed you in ways you can't even imagine. Have you chosen Him? It breaks His heart when the ones He has chosen refuse to choose Him.

> O Jerusalem, Jerusalem, which killest the prophets, and stonest them that are sent unto thee; how often would I have gathered thy children together, as a hen doth gather her brood under her wings, and ye would not!
>
> Luke 13:34

God chose you, and if you have not accepted Him, the following accusation will be waiting for you in the judgment.

> Because I have called, and ye refused; I have stretched out my hand, and no man regarded; but ye

have set at nought all my counsel, and would none of my reproof: I also will laugh at your calamity; I will mock when your fear cometh; when your fear cometh as desolation, and your destruction cometh as a whirlwind; when distress and anguish cometh upon you. Then shall they call upon me, but I will not answer; they shall seek me early, but they shall not find me: for that they hated knowledge, and did not choose the fear of the LORD.

Proverbs 1:24–29

God chose you. Don't neglect to accept Him.

Something to Think About

When people finally make up their minds to live for God, their response is immediate. Salvation is more important than anything else in their lives. Time is of utmost importance because once it's gone, we can't get it back. God says the time is NOW. Look at how the following people responded to the gospel:

- Acts 2:41–42: After Peter preached on the Day of Pentecost, three thousand people were baptized that same day.
- Acts 8:12–13: As soon as the Samaritans heard Philip's exhortation, they believed and were baptized.
- Acts 8:35–38 (NET Bible): The Ethiopian eunuch believed Philip's teaching and exclaimed, "Look, there is water! What is to stop me from being baptized?"

Jesus Made The Choice

- Acts 9:18: When Ananias prayed for Paul, he regained his sight and was baptized "forthwith" (without delay).
- Acts 10:47–48: Peter commanded the believers in Cornelius's house to be baptized, and they immediately obeyed.
- Acts 16:14–15: Lydia listened intently to Paul's teaching. She opened her heart to the Lord, and she and her household were baptized.
- Acts 16:33: Paul and Silas witnessed to the Philippian jailer, and baptized him and his house that same hour. It was a time of rejoicing!

Acts 24:25 tells a different story involving Felix, a Roman governor of Judea, who had married a Jewess named Drusilla. The New Living Testament says Felix was "quite familiar with the Way," but after hearing Paul, he quickly adjourned the meeting, saying he would wait until the chief captain arrived to corroborate Paul's claims. But curiosity overcame him, and he summoned Paul out of the prison. He and Drusilla listened intently to Paul's testimony concerning faith in Christ. Greatly impacted, Felix trembled but couldn't quite bring himself to commit. He said, "That's enough for now! You may leave. When I find it convenient, I will send for you [again]" (Acts 24:25, NIV). But he never did.

Chapter Eleven

The Great Confirmation

Have you ever read a book that began with a prologue of events leading up to the subject of the story? I recently read a novel about the Civil War. It didn't start with the beginning of the war but with the political upheaval and rising tensions prior to the election of Abraham Lincoln. The actual conflict did not start until several chapters into the book.

I submit that in like manner, the New Testament does not begin with Matthew's Gospel, but several books later in the book of Acts. For me, the narrations in the Gospels are like a vital prologue that leads up to the initiation of the Lord's New Testament church. Matthew, Mark, Luke, and John contain biographies of Christ. They tell of His birth, ministry, crucifixion, death, and resurrection. Although Jesus spoke of salvation in the Gospels, it is in the New Testament—beginning with the book of Acts—that we find the confirmation of what He said by the eyewitnesses that heard Him.

The New Testament, which Jesus initiated with the breaking of His body and the shedding of His blood, could not take effect until after His death.

Chapter Eleven

For where a testament is, there must also of necessity be the death of the testator. For a testament is of force after men are dead: otherwise it is of no strength at all while the testator liveth.

Hebrews 9:16–17

It wasn't until the outpouring of God's Holy Spirit on the Day of Pentecost that the New Testament began. Acts 2 recounts the beginning of the New Testament church.

Jesus spoke of salvation. He proclaimed that whosoever believes and is baptized will be saved. In John 3, He said that without exception one must be born of the water and of the Spirit in order to enter the kingdom of God. At His ascension, He left instructions that all nations must be taught, baptized, and instructed on how to live godly in this present world.

He left it to those that heard Him to confirm what He said. To confirm means to verify, to make proof of, to show evidence of, to prove as accurate, as well as to establish the correctness of something previously believed. This was the mission of the apostles.

When the religious critics confronted the Lord, asking Him of his doctrine, He replied, "Why do you ask me? Ask those who heard what I said. They know what I said" (John 18:21, NET).

The Great Confirmation

In the desperate prayer of passion in the Garden of Gethsemane, the Lord prayed for His disciples and their mission after His crucifixion, and then He prayed for us. "I am not praying only on their behalf, but also on behalf of those who believe in me through their [the apostles'] testimony" (John 17:20). It was to be through the confirmation of those who had heard Him.

"Then he opened their [the disciples'] minds to understand the Scriptures" (Luke 24:45, ESV). The disciples were given a divine understanding and revelation of what the Lord spoke concerning salvation. We are to believe on Jesus, not according to church traditions, religious professors, televangelists, or anyone else, but through what the apostles taught. It must be through their word (testimony).

> We are of God: he that knoweth God heareth us; he that is not of God heareth not us. Hereby know we the spirit of truth, and the spirit of error.
>
> I John 4:6

Are you following the Catholics, the Lutherans, the Baptists, the Church of God in Christ, Seventh Day Adventists, or any number of other religious groups? Or are you following those who confirmed His Word—the apostles?

> And they continued stedfastly in the apostles' doctrine and fellowship, and in breaking of bread, and in prayers.
>
> Acts 2:42

Chapter Eleven

What shall we do to be saved? That is an important question. It is a biblical question. A biblical question deserves a biblical answer. The answer is always the same:

> Now when they heard this, they were pricked in their heart, and said unto Peter and to the rest of the apostles, Men and brethren, what shall we do? Then Peter said unto them, Repent, and be baptized every one of you in the name of Jesus Christ for the remission of sins, and ye shall receive the gift of the Holy Ghost.
>
> Acts 2:37–38

> He that believeth on me, as the scripture hath said, out of his belly shall flow rivers of living water.
>
> John 7:38

Because we adhere to the Scriptures and refuse to conform to religious traditions, we have been labeled false teachers, a cult, the "New Issue," and "Jesus only." Some have even called us heretics. However, we choose to stand with the teachings of the apostles.

> But this I confess unto thee, that after the way which they call heresy, so worship I the God of my fathers, believing all things which are written in the law and in the prophets.
>
> Acts 24:14

The Great Confirmation

It was foretold that the time would come when some would no longer endure sound doctrine, and would depart from the faith, exchanging truth for error (I Timothy 4:1–5; II Timothy 3:1; 4:1–4). "For laying aside the commandment of God, ye hold the tradition of men" (Mark 7:8).

Something to Think About

When you take a stand, whose side will you be on?

> Then came one and told them, saying, Behold, the men whom ye put in prison are standing in the temple, and teaching the people. Then went the captain with the officers, and brought them without violence: for they feared the people, lest they should have been stoned. And when they had brought them, they set them before the council: and the high priest asked them, Saying, Did not we straitly command you that ye should not teach in this name? and, behold, ye have filled Jerusalem with your doctrine, and intend to bring this man's blood upon us. Then Peter and the other apostles answered and said, We ought to obey God rather than men.
>
> Acts 5:25–29

When the religious people brought the apostles before the council, their number-one problem—the huge stumbling block—was the NAME. They accused the apostles of being people of the Name and of filling the city with the doctrine of Christ. Although the accusers probably didn't realize it (and would have been appalled if they had), there was a great revelation in their fear of the Name. You see, it's the Name that brings the blood, and it's the blood that brings remission of sin. The devil hates the Name. Religious tradition rejects the Name in baptism, but I stand with the apostles: "We ought to obey God rather than men."

Chapter Twelve

The Traditions of Men

Were you aware that the baptismal formula using the name of Jesus Christ was changed to using only the titles Father, Son, and Holy Ghost by the Catholic Church?

Britannica Encyclopedia, 11th ed., vol. 3 (pg. 365)—The baptismal formula was changed from the name of Jesus to words "Father, Son, and Holy Ghost in 2nd century.

Canney Encyclopedia of Religion (pg. 53)—The early church baptized in the name of the Lord Jesus until the development of the Trinitarian doctrine in the second century.

New International Encyclopedia, vol. 2 (pg. 263)—The term "Trinity" was originated by Tertullian, a Roman Catholic Church Father.

Hastings Encyclopedia of Religion, vol. 2 (pg. 377)—Christian baptism was administered using the words "in the name of Jesus." Baptism was always in the name of Jesus until the time of Justin Martyr (p. 389).

Catholic Encyclopedia, vol. 2, (pg. 263)—Here the Catholic authors acknowledged that the baptismal formula was changed by their church.

Schaff-Herzog Religious Encyclopedia, vol. 1 (pg. 435)—The New Testament knows only the baptism in the name of Jesus.

Hastings Dictionary of the Bible (pg. 88)—It must be acknowledged that the threefold name of Matthew 28:19 does not appear to have been used by the primitive church, but rather in the name of Jesus, Jesus Christ or Lord Jesus.

Note: to find a more complete list of proofs, see "The History of Baptism in Jesus' Name," The Apostolic Archives International Incorporated at:

ttps://www.apostolicarchives.com/articles/article/8801925/180090.htm.

The Traditions Of Men

Matthew 28:19 was a command by Jesus to baptize in a Name. The apostles did not repeat the words of the command; they obeyed it! Since "Father, Son, and Holy Ghost" are titles of the manifestations of Almighty God, the apostles understood His saving name to be Jesus. Can any dare say that the apostles disobeyed the Lord or failed to baptize properly? Jesus had spent forty days after His resurrection with the apostles, during which time He opened their understanding that they might understand the Scriptures. (See Luke 24:45.) They knew precisely and accurately the formula for baptism, and it was not in the name of the Father and of the Son and of the Holy Ghost. It is in the name of Jesus! The actions of the apostles in the book of Acts prove this to be true. Invariably, at every baptismal service recorded in the book of Acts, the apostles and evangelists baptized converts in the name of Jesus Christ for the remission of sins.

Do you still refuse to be baptized in the name of the Lord Jesus Christ? The only conclusion for that is that you love darkness, false religion, and tradition of men more than the light of the glorious gospel. This bold statement was confirmed by the words of Jesus:

> For God sent not his Son into the world to condemn the world; but that the world through him might be saved. He that believeth on him is not condemned: but he that believeth not is condemned already, because he hath not believed in the name of the only begotten Son of God. And this is the condemnation, that light is come into the world, and men loved

darkness rather than light, because their deeds were evil. For every one that doeth evil hateth the light, neither cometh to the light, lest his deeds should be reproved. But he that doeth truth cometh to the light, that his deeds may be made manifest, that they are wrought in God.

John 3:17–21

There are no other alternatives to being born again the right way; it is a must.

If we this day be examined of the good deed done to the impotent man, by what means he is made whole; be it known unto you all, and to all the people of Israel, that by the name of Jesus Christ of Nazareth, whom ye crucified, whom God raised from the dead, even by him doth this man stand here before you whole. This is the stone which was set at nought of you builders, which is become the head of the corner. Neither is there salvation in any other: for there is none other name under heaven given among men, whereby we must be saved.

Acts 4:9–12

The Bible says Peter was "filled with the Holy Ghost" as he spoke to the priests, the captain of the Temple, and the Sadducees, saying this gospel was known "unto you all." Today the gospel of Jesus Christ is still being preached and taught. It is still "known

The Traditions Of Men

unto you all." Yet many set this gospel of Jesus Christ aside, ignore it, and simply refuse to obey it. Others would rather not know, as knowledge would require a change they are not willing to make. God promised to all of us that somewhere on our journey through life, the grace that brings salvation will appear to every one of us. Take heed how you receive this truth.

> For it had been better for them not to have known the way of righteousness, than, after they have known it, to turn from the holy commandment delivered unto them.
>
> II Peter 2:21

These things you NOW know.

Comments by the Author

Mankind is naturally religious; he will always worship something. But mankind is also naturally rebellious; he will do what he wants. The result is that when it comes to religion, people often do the right thing in the wrong way. And when they are shown what is right, they get offended and find a church that fits their way of thinking. Being born again is the right thing to do, but many do it the wrong way. Some ignore it, others don't study it, and many don't even question what they have been taught. But as Jesus said in John 3:3–6, if a person has not been born again, he or she won't see the kingdom of God. It is not hard to see the kingdom or to find the right way to get there. If the way is hidden, it is hidden in plain sight. It is my hope and prayer that this book will show you the right way and help you discover the truths you ought to know.

Mike Easter

About the Author

In 1981 at the age of 26 years old, Michael Easter surrendered to the call of God and repented of his sins. He was baptized on his birthday signifying his new birth into the Kingdom of God.

Those early days included responsibilities as the church worship leader, audio-visual director, and Sunday school superintendent. Brother Easter was passionate about the work of God and taught Home Bible Studies to friends and relatives, winning many to the Lord.

Because of his faithfulness, God used him to win his parents and sisters to the truth.

Family Life

Mike was married to Portia Whetzel in May 1988 in Newport News, VA. They worked together in their church, The United Pentecostal Church, under the leadership of their pastor, Rev. Jack Cunningham. While Mike joined the ministry team, Portia successfully coached the Bible Quiz team, a group of young children and teenagers memorizing hundreds of scriptures to several consecutive district championships.

During this time, Mike and Portia became proud parents of daughter, Bethany (1991) and son, Jordan (1995). They presently reside in Newport News and attend The Peninsula Pentecostals pastored by Rev. Jared Arango.

The Evangelistic Call

Content to serve in any capacity, God promoted Michael in 1992 from the local church Sunday school ministry to the office of Virginia District Sunday School Secretary. After a term in that office, he was elected to District Sunday School Director for 8 years. It was during this tenure that Mike was able to travel and minister, preaching and teaching seminars across the country.

In 1994, Michael entered the full-time ministry as the assistant pastor working along side Pastor Jared Arango in an aggressive revival church in Newport News.

God's grace was mightily upon him as he was granted favor with God and man. His ministry was in demand and the calls for his ministry greatly multiplied.

Michael responded in faith in the the year 2000 and entered the evangelistic field traveling exclusively throughout North America.

Current Ministry

Since 2000.... It has been a whirlwind of apostolic power and revival. Hundreds have been baptized and multitudes filled with the baptism of the Holy Ghost. Mike Easter's ministry is encouraging, refreshing, and dynamic. God has anointed his servant to preach this soul saving gospel.

He authored his first book, an insightful handbook for new evangelists titled "You Dont Have to Wait 'Til Spring to Have an Easter Revival!".

You may contact him at: MLEastr@aol.com

Michael and Portia Easter